For Professor Harish Chander and Vijay Kumari — present in every word I write.

First Edition

ISBN: 978-93-344-0230-8

Cover Design: Designed by the author
Publisher: Self-published

For permissions, inquiries, or to request group or institutional access:
[satishchandra@galileolabs.in, satishchandra.sr@gmail.com]

Foreword

The rise of artificial intelligence marks one of the most transformative shifts in human history. Just as electricity once reshaped industries and the internet redefined connectivity, AI is rapidly becoming the invisible force driving innovation across every domain. Yet, at the heart of this revolution lies a deceptively simple truth: the quality of what we get from AI depends profoundly on how we ask for it.

This is where the discipline of prompt engineering emerges — not merely as a technical skill, but as an art form. The ability to craft precise, creative, and strategic prompts determines whether AI becomes a blunt tool or a refined instrument of progress.

In The *Art of Prompt Engineering — Unlocking AI's Full Potential, by Satish Chandra* provides readers with far more than a collection of tips and tricks. This book is a roadmap to understanding how language interacts with intelligence — both human and artificial. It explores the nuances of framing, context, and creativity, empowering readers to bridge the gap between what they imagine and what AI can deliver.

What excites me most about this work is its accessibility. Whether you are a researcher, educator, entrepreneur, or simply an enthusiast curious about AI, this book equips you with practical techniques to harness its power responsibly and effectively. More importantly, it reminds us that AI is not here to replace human ingenuity — it is here to amplify it.

As you turn these pages, you will discover that prompt engineering is more than technical mastery; it is about cultivating clarity of thought, precision of expression, and the courage to experiment. In this journey, you are not just learning to speak with machines — you are learning to unlock new dimensions of your own creativity.

I invite you to dive into this book with curiosity and imagination. The future belongs to those who know how to ask the right questions.

Dr. Arvind Rao, PhD
Professor of Artificial Intelligence and Human-Machine Interaction

Preface

The story of this book begins with a simple realization: artificial intelligence is only as powerful as the instructions it receives. When I first started experimenting with large language models and generative AI, I was both fascinated and frustrated. Fascinated by the sheer range of possibilities, yet frustrated by how dramatically the outcomes varied depending on the way I phrased a question. A single word, a shift in tone, or a touch of added context could change the result from ordinary to extraordinary.

That experience sparked a deeper exploration into what we now call **prompt engineering** — the deliberate practice of designing inputs that guide AI systems toward meaningful, accurate, and creative outputs. It became clear to me that this skill was more than a technical curiosity; it was the key to unlocking AI's true potential across industries, professions, and personal creativity.

This book is the product of that journey. It is not intended solely for engineers or researchers, but for anyone who wishes to communicate more effectively with AI. Entrepreneurs will find strategies for building innovative tools and services. Educators will discover ways to create engaging learning experiences. Writers, artists, and creators will see how AI can become a partner in imagination. And everyday users will learn how to transform AI from a novelty into a reliable assistant.

Throughout these chapters, I aim to balance the practical and the conceptual. You will encounter actionable frameworks, tested prompt templates, and real-world applications, but also reflections on the evolving relationship between humans and intelligent machines. My hope is that you come away not just with better results from AI, but with a clearer appreciation of how language shapes intelligence itself.

As you read, I encourage you to approach prompt engineering with curiosity, experimentation, and creativity. There is no single "perfect" prompt — only endless opportunities to refine your interaction and push the boundaries of what's possible.

May this book serve as both a guide and an invitation: a guide to mastering the craft of prompt engineering, and an invitation to explore a future where humans and AI collaborate in extraordinary ways.

Satish Chandra, Author

Acknowledgment & Thank You

I would like to express my deepest gratitude to my family, whose love and support have been the true foundation of this journey.

To my in-laws, Mrs. & Mr. Indra Jalla and Sanjai Jalla, thank you for your encouragement, blessings, and unwavering belief in me. Your guidance and warmth have been a source of strength throughout this endeavour.

To my beloved wife, Shalini, your patience, understanding, and constant support have made this work possible. You have been my anchor and my inspiration, reminding me to keep moving forward even when the path seemed uncertain.

To my wonderful sons, Bhavya and Rudra, you bring joy, laughter, and purpose to my life every single day. This book is also a dedication to your future, where imagination and learning will always have a place.

And to my ever-loyal companion, Zinaida, our cat — thank you for the quiet comfort, warmth, and playful moments that brightened my days while writing.

This book would not have been possible without each of you.

With love and gratitude,

Satish Chandra

How To Use This Book

This book is a practical guide, not just theory. Use it as a **toolbox** you can open whenever you need it.

1. **Start with the basics.**

If you're new to AI, begin with **Part I: Foundations**. These chapters explain prompts in simple terms, with examples and exercises to help you practice.

2. **Learn by doing.**

At the end of each chapter, you'll find **exercises**. Treat them as experiments. Try them out with your favourite AI tool — you'll learn faster by applying ideas immediately.

3. **Jump to what matters most.**

You don't have to read in order. Use the table of contents like a map:

- **Business & Education** — practical use cases.
- **Creative Writing & Content** — storytelling, blogging, and ideation.
- **Software Development** — coding help and debugging.
- **Visual & Multimodal AI** — prompts for images, video, and more.

4. **Explore techniques.**

Part II and III focus on practical prompting with ChatGPT, Claude, and image models like DALL·E or Midjourney. These chapters show you how to refine prompts for consistency, creativity, and accuracy.

5. **Keep the reference tools handy.**

Toward the back, you'll find **prompt templates, tools, and model comparisons**. These sections are designed for quick look-up whenever you need inspiration or structure.

6. **Think about the bigger picture.**

Part V highlights common mistakes, ethical concerns, and the future of prompting. These chapters will help you use AI thoughtfully and responsibly.

Key tip: Don't just read — **experiment**. AI responds best to curiosity, clarity, and creativity. The more you practice, the more powerful your results will become.

Contents

AI: Your Friendly Neighbourhood Thinking Machine

Artificial intelligence, or AI, is no longer a futuristic concept from science fiction. It is quietly woven into the technology we use every day — whether it's your phone recognizing faces in photos, a streaming service suggesting your next movie, or an assistant that responds when you call its name. In simple terms, AI gives computers a measure of "intelligence," allowing them to perform tasks that once required human judgment or learning.

A Brief History of the Dream

The idea of intelligent machines is older than modern computing. Ancient myths imagined lifelike beings such as Talos, a bronze giant from Greek legend. In the 20th century, mathematician Alan Turing posed the famous question: *"Can machines think?"* His challenge laid the foundation for what became known as artificial intelligence.

In 1956, a group of scientists at Dartmouth formally named the field. Early experiments showed promise: programs that could play checkers, solve puzzles, or simulate a simple conversation. One of the first chatbots, ELIZA, created in the 1960s, mimicked a therapist by reflecting users' words back to them. Though rudimentary, it revealed how people could form emotional connections with even the simplest simulations of understanding.

The journey was not always smooth. Expectations in the 1960s and '70s were high, but progress was slower than anticipated. Funding dried up, leading to periods known as "AI winters." Yet advances in computing power, coupled with new methods such as deep learning in the 2010s, reignited the field. Today, AI is not only back — it is everywhere.

How Does AI Learn?

At its core, AI learns by finding patterns in data. Suppose you want an AI system to recognize apples. You show it thousands of labelled examples — some apples, some not. Over time, the system detects recurring features:

round shapes, smooth skin, shades of red or green, a small stem. Eventually, it can identify apples it has never seen before.

This process relies on **neural networks**; digital structures inspired loosely by the human brain. Each "neuron" processes a small piece of information and passes it along, gradually refining the system's ability to classify or predict. By adjusting these internal connections — known as weights — the AI improves its performance, much like a student who learns from mistakes and corrections.

AI in Everyday Life

Far from being hidden in laboratories, AI now shapes daily experiences:

- **Navigation**: Apps like Google Maps analyse traffic data to suggest the fastest route.
- **Face recognition**: Your phone unlocks when it recognizes you.
- **Language tools**: Autocorrect and translation apps quietly assist with writing and communication.
- **Recommendations**: Platforms such as YouTube, Spotify, and Netflix analyse your activity to predict what you'll enjoy next.
- **Virtual assistants**: Siri, Alexa, and other chatbots respond to commands and questions.
- **Games**: AI powers realistic opponents that adapt to your strategies.

Often invisible, AI serves as the hidden helper behind countless conveniences.

The Creative and Curious Side of AI

AI is not just practical — it is also imaginative. Systems can generate art, music, and stories, sometimes producing results that surprise even their creators. In competitive arenas, AI has achieved remarkable victories, defeating world champions in games such as chess and Go. At the same time, it can still make glaring mistakes: mislabelling an image or offering a nonsensical answer with great confidence. These quirks remind us that while AI is powerful, it is far from infallible.

Looking Ahead

Where does AI go from here? Today's systems are considered "narrow AI" — highly skilled at specific tasks, but unable to match the broad flexibility of human intelligence. The vision of *artificial general intelligence* (AGI), machines that can reason across many domains as we do, remains hypothetical.

More immediate questions concern how we will use the tools we already have. Will automation replace certain jobs, and what new roles might emerge? Can we address bias in AI systems to ensure fairness? How do we safeguard against misuse while promoting innovation? These are not just technical challenges, but societal ones.

Conclusion

AI is not a rival to human intelligence — it is a tool, as transformative as electricity or the internet. Like any tool, it requires thoughtful use. When guided well, it can support breakthroughs in medicine, help address climate change, or assist in education and creativity. When misused or misunderstood, it can create risks.

The future of AI is still being written. It may help cure diseases, explore space, or simply refine how we communicate online. What is certain is that it will remain part of our daily lives. The more we understand how it works and what it can — and cannot — do, the better we can shape it into something that benefits us all.

End of Chapter Exercises

1. Which ancient myth is mentioned in the text as an early example of humans imagining a "thinking machine"?

   A) Pandora's Box

   B) Talos, the bronze man

   C) Minotaur of Crete

   D) Pygmalion's statue

2. What event in 1956 is marked as the official naming of the field "artificial intelligence"?

   A) Alan Turing publishing his test

   B) Creation of the first AI checkers program

   C) Dartmouth College summer conference

   D) The invention of ELIZA

3. Arthur Samuel's checkers program was historically important because:

   A) It played checkers faster than humans.

   B) It was the first program to mimic therapy sessions.

   C) It could learn and improve beyond its programmer's skill.

   D) It predicted human-level AI in a few decades.

4. ELIZA, created in the 1960s, is significant because:

   A) It was the first program to beat humans at Go.

   B) It pretended to be a therapist through text conversation.

   C) It demonstrated deep learning neural networks.

   D) It was the first AI winter project.

5. Which of the following best describes an AI "neural network" according to the text?
   A) A fixed set of instructions for solving logical problems
   B) A network of "digital brain cells" that pass signals and adjust weights
   C) A random generator of possible outcomes from data
   D) A type of hardware chip specialized for calculations

6. In the analogy comparing AI to a chef, what do "ingredients" represent?
   A) Feedback signals
   B) Algorithms
   C) Data
   D) Neural connections

7. Which breakthrough in the 2010s reignited AI progress, according to the text?
   A) Symbolic logic
   B) Deep learning
   C) ELIZA-style chatbots
   D) Genetic algorithms

8. The text compares GPT models to which of the following?
   A) A genius parrot
   B) A chess grandmaster
   C) An infinite library
   D) A scientist-in-training

9. Which of the following is **NOT** given as a current example of AI use in everyday life?
   A) Spam filters in email
   B) Traffic navigation in maps

C) Predicting weather patterns centuries ahead

D) Virtual filters for faces in photos

10. What term is used for the idea of a machine with human-level general intelligence?

    A) Deep AI

    B) AGI (Artificial General Intelligence)

    C) Machine Autonomy

    D) Cognitive Robotics

Part I: Foundations of Prompt Engineering

1. What Is an AI Prompt?

In AI, a prompt is simply the input or instruction you give to an artificial intelligence model to tell it what you want. In practice, this is usually text. For example, a prompt might be a question, a command, or any description of the task. As TechTarget.com explains, "an AI prompt is the input submitted to a large language model" - it can be a question, command, statement, code sample, etcetera. Similarly, an educational glossary, flintk12.com, defines a prompt as "a piece of text, question, or instruction given to an AI system...to trigger a specific response or action". In other words, when you use something like ChatGPT, whatever you type in is your prompt. Imagine talking to a very clever robot or genie. The words or question you say out loud (or type) is the prompt. One teacher put it this way: "A prompt is what you say to the computer to tell it what you want. Just like you ask your teacher a question, you ask the computer something, and it gives you an answer.". In that analogy, you are like the student asking the question, and the AI is like the teacher that responds.

How Does the AI Use the Prompt?

When you give a prompt to a language model (like ChatGPT), the model takes that text as its starting point and then generates a response word by word. Under the hood, the AI has learned patterns from billions of examples of text. When it sees your prompt, it "predicts" what comes next in a way that seems like the answer. In simple terms, the prompt provides context and instructions for the model's response. As TechTarget notes, once the prompt is submitted, the AI "uses the input as a foundation for generating an appropriate response".

Think of it as a very advanced autocomplete. If you start typing a story on your phone, the autocomplete suggests how to finish the sentence. An AI model does something similar, but on steroids: your prompt is the beginning of the story (or question), and the AI tries to continue it in a way that makes sense. For instance, if your prompt is "Tell me a funny story about a robot learning to cook," the AI will try to continue and write a funny robot story. If your prompt is "Solve 2+2," it will answer "4."

Another analogy: imagine the AI as an extremely capable but very literal personal assistant. If you just say "do something," the assistant will be confused. If you clearly say, "Please write a thank-you email to my friend from the party," the assistant will know exactly what to do. One writer describes an AI prompt as giving "really clear instructions to an incredibly capable, but very literal-minded personal assistant.". In short, the better and clearer the prompt, the better and more focused the AI's answer will be.

Why Does Prompt Wording Matter?

The exact words and details in your prompt have a big impact on the AI's output. An AI model can give very different answers depending on how you ask. If your prompt is vague, the answer will also be vague or generic. If your prompt is specific and detailed, the answer will be more precise and on-topic. In fact, experts note that the prompt's goal is to give the AI exactly the information it needs for an accurate answer. In other words, the prompt guides the AI.

For example, the same question phrased differently will yield different results. Flint's educator guide points out that "a vague prompt might lead to an irrelevant or generic answer. A clear and specific prompt, on the other hand, produces a focused and often more accurate result.". This is just like homework: if your teacher's assignment says "write something about animals," you might write anything. But if the assignment is "write a paragraph about how elephants use their trunks to drink water," you'll get a much better answer.

Another everyday analogy is a recipe. A cooking recipe works best when you list clear ingredients and steps. Saying "make food" is too vague; the chef won't know what you want. Similarly, a good prompt is like a detailed recipe for the AI. The more context or constraints you give (like style, format, or examples), the more the AI can "cook up" a suitable answer.

Additionally, the AI uses its training to interpret your prompt. Large language models have been trained on huge datasets of text. When they see your prompt, they look for patterns similar to that text in their training and follow those patterns. So, if you say "Write a poem about summer," the AI will recall how poems sound and try to create one. If you say "Explain photosynthesis to a 5th grader," it will adjust its explanation to be simpler.

Prompts Are Like Conversations with a Super-Helpful Friend

A fun way to think of prompts is like chatting with a friendly helper or tutor. If you ask your smart friend, "How do I fix this math problem?" that question is your prompt. The friend will answer based on the question. If you say "math problem" only, your friend won't know which one. But if you say "How do I solve 7×8?", you'll get a clear answer (56). The same goes for AI: being clear in the prompt helps it know exactly what to do.

Likewise, if you say, "Tell me about science," the AI might give a very long and general answer. But if you say, "Explain Newton's first law of motion in simple terms," the AI will tailor its answer to that topic and audience. One analogy from teachers is: you're giving instructions to the AI, like a teacher would to a student. The clearer the instructions, the better the student (AI) performs.

Finally, remember that prompts don't just work for text. Many image-generation AIs (like DALL·E or Stable Diffusion) also use text prompts. In those cases, the prompt is the description of the picture you want. For example, a famous demo of Stable Diffusion used the same text prompt to generate nine anime pictures. The result (shown below) has all the images sharing a very similar style and subject, because the prompt was identical . (This illustrates how the prompt steers the AI's output even in images.)

For example, these nine anime-style images were all generated from a single text prompt. Since the prompt was the same, the images have a consistent style and theme.

Examples of Good and Bad Prompts

To see how prompt wording matters, here are some examples:

- **Vague vs. Specific (School Essay):**
  - **Bad prompt:** "Tell me about school." (very general)
  - **Better prompt:** "Write a paragraph about what a typical school day is like for a fifth grader in the United States."

The first prompt ("Tell me about school.") is too open-ended, so the AI might give a short or unfocused answer. The second prompt has a clear topic and audience, so the AI can produce a detailed, relevant paragraph

.

- **Simple vs. Detailed (Travel Planning):**
  - **Bad prompt:** "I want to go on holiday. Where should I go?" (very short and broad)

- **Better prompt:** "Acting as a travel planner, plan a 3-day family trip to Paris with kid-friendly activities. Create an itinerary with daily schedules and recommend a hotel."

The first prompt simply asks "Where should I go?" which is too vague. The second prompt specifies location (Paris), duration (3-day), group (family with kids), and even asks for an itinerary and hotel. As a result, the AI can give a detailed travel plan rather than a one-word answer.

- **General vs. Detailed (Cooking Recipe):**
  - **Bad prompt:** "I want to cook something." (too minimal)
  - **Better prompt:** "Acting as an expert home cook, recommend a recipe for vegetarian Italian food that can be prepared in 30 minutes. Include a list of ingredients and step-by-step instructions."

The first prompt is too broad. The improved prompt adds the role ("expert home cook"), the cuisine (Italian, vegetarian), and a time limit (30 minutes). This extra detail helps the AI know exactly what kind of recipe to suggest.

These examples show how adding context, details, or a clear role makes prompts much more effective. In each case, the good prompt guides the AI to produce a better answer.

Key Takeaways

- A prompt is the text input you give an AI (usually a language model) that tells it what you want. It can be a question, instruction, or any text.

- The AI treats the prompt as the starting point and generates its response based on it. The clearer and more specific the prompt, the more accurate and useful the response.

- Think of prompts like instructions for a friend or assistant. If you tell your friend exactly what you need, they'll help much better than if you stay vague.

- Good prompts usually include enough context, detail, and a clear question or task. Vague prompts often lead to vague answers.

By practicing clear, well-phrased prompts (almost like being a good interviewer or writer of instructions), you'll find AI tools give you much better and more relevant outputs. Start with a simple prompt and then add more detail or examples if the answer isn't quite what you need. Happy prompting!

End of Chapter Exercises

1. According to TechTarget, what is an AI prompt?

   A) A sequence of outputs generated by a neural network

   B) The training data used to improve a large language model

   C) The input submitted to a large language model, such as a question or command

   D) A specialized algorithm that interprets user intent

2. Which analogy in the text compares prompting AI to a classroom scenario?

   A) Student writing an exam while teacher grades

   B) Student asking a question, teacher responding

   C) Teacher giving vague assignments to students

   D) Students copying from a textbook

3. What mechanism is used by AI models like ChatGPT to generate responses after receiving a prompt?

   A) Random sampling of internet content

   B) Predicting the next word based on patterns from training data

   C) Matching the input to pre-programmed answers

   D) Logical deduction through symbolic reasoning

4. Which description best matches the "personal assistant" analogy of prompting?

   A) A creative assistant who improvises tasks with minimal direction

   B) A literal-minded but capable assistant who needs very clear instructions

   C) A disobedient assistant who resists vague orders

   D) A playful assistant who offers random suggestions

5. Why does the text compare good prompts to recipes?

   A) Recipes are always vague and AI learns to interpret them

   B) Recipes show that generic steps can still lead to useful outcomes

   C) Recipes illustrate the importance of precise ingredients and steps for accurate results

   D) Recipes highlight that cooking and AI both rely on random guesses

6. Which of the following is NOT an example used in the text to illustrate good vs. bad prompts?

   A) School essay writing

   B) Travel planning

   C) Cooking a recipe

   D) Medical diagnosis

7. Why does the text say vague prompts often fail?

   A) Because AI ignores unclear instructions completely

   B) Because vague prompts make AI retrieve irrelevant or generic answers

   C) Because vague prompts overload the AI's training data

   D) Because vague prompts increase AI's processing time

8. Which example demonstrates role-based prompting as described in the text?

   A) "Tell me about animals."

   B) "Write something about school."

   C) "Acting as a travel planner, plan a 3-day family trip to Paris."

   D) "Explain science."

9. What was demonstrated by Stable Diffusion's nine anime images generated from the same prompt?

   A) AI cannot maintain consistency across multiple outputs

B) Identical prompts lead to consistent style and subject in results

C) AI generates random artistic variations regardless of input

D) Prompts only influence text, not images

10. Which key takeaway from the text best summarizes the role of prompts?

    A) Prompts restrict AI's creativity and should be avoided

    B) Prompts are only useful for text generation, not images

    C) Clear, specific prompts guide AI toward accurate and useful responses

    D) Prompts are irrelevant since AI already knows what the user wants

2. What is Prompt Engineering?

Imagine talking to a super smart robot. How you ask it things makes a big difference! In AI, a prompt is simply what you say or type to the robot (AI model) to get an answer. Prompt engineering is the art of writing those prompts clearly and carefully so the AI gives the output you want. In other words, it's the step-by-step process of creating inputs (prompts) that shape the AI's output. If you give good, detailed instructions, the AI will give a useful answer. If your prompt is vague or confusing, the AI might give a strange or wrong response.

Think of the AI as a student or helper that you need to guide. You're basically "programming with words": instead of writing code, you write a clear question or command. By choosing the right words and examples, you steer the AI toward the desired answer. As one guide puts it, prompt engineering is "the art and science of designing and optimizing prompts". It often takes some creativity and practice — like finding the perfect wording — to get the best results from the AI.

Why Is Prompt Engineering Important?

- **Clear answers:** AI needs context and details. Good prompts give it enough information so it can produce accurate, relevant responses. For example, simply asking "Tell me about cats" might get a short answer, but asking "Share three fun facts about cats in a friendly tone" guides the AI to a better answer.

- **User control:** Well-crafted prompts let you steer the AI. By specifying style or role (e.g. "Explain this like a teacher" or "Use bullet points"), you can guide how the AI replies. Effective prompts provide intent and context to refine the AI's output.

- **Efficiency (First-try success):** Writing good prompts often means you get the right answer on the first try. This saves time and avoids endless trial-and-error. As AWS notes, prompt engineering helps users "avoid trial and error and still receive coherent, accurate, and relevant responses" on the first prompt.

- **Better AI performance:** Overall, prompting the AI well makes it more useful. AWS explains that prompt engineering makes AI systems more efficient and effective. Instead of vague requests that confuse the AI, clear prompts turn the AI's power into meaningful, usable outputs.

By spending a little extra effort on how you ask, you get better answers and more reliable AI help.

Prompt Engineering in Everyday Terms

Imagine an AI as a friendly robot teacher. To get a good lesson, you need to ask clear questions. Prompt engineering is like giving instructions to that robot so it doesn't get confused. One story says it's "like giving instructions to an over-eager genie": if your instructions are too vague, the genie (AI) will give you crazy results, but if they're just right, magic happens and you get exactly what you want.

Another analogy: asking a child to pack you lunch. If you just say "Make me something tasty," you might end up with a plain ketchup sandwich. But if you say, "Pack me a turkey sandwich, an apple, and some carrot sticks," you'll get a great meal. Writing prompts for AI works the same way - the more details you give, the closer the result is to what you wanted.

Examples: Basic vs. Engineered Prompts

Basic prompt: "Write a story about a cat."
Better prompt: "Write a short, funny story about a clever cat and a playful dog who become best friends."
Why it helps: The improved prompt adds specifics (tone, characters), so the AI knows exactly what kind of story to create.

Basic prompt: "Explain photosynthesis."
Better prompt: "Explain photosynthesis in simple words, as if you're teaching a curious 10-year-old, using a water-cycle analogy."
Why it helps: This prompt tells the AI the audience (a 10-year-old) and style (simple, with an analogy), so the explanation will be easier to understand.

Basic prompt: "Give me recipe."
Better prompt: "List the ingredients and steps for an easy pasta recipe for beginners, including cooking tips."
Why it helps: By specifying "for beginners" and "include steps," the AI will give a clear, helpful recipe rather than just naming ingredients.

Each example shows how adding context, detail, or instructions turns a generic question into a specific one that guides the AI to a great answer. Prompt engineering might sound fancy, but it's really just about being clear and creative with your questions. With a little practice, anyone can learn to write better prompts. Now you know the basics – it's time to have fun asking questions and seeing what amazing answers you can get!

The Rise of Large Language Models

Hello there, curious minds!

Today, we're going on an exciting journey into one of the coolest things happening in technology right now — the rise of large language models, or LLMs for short. Don't worry, that might sound like a mouthful, but I'll break it down in a way that even your younger cousin could understand.

What's a Large Language Model?

Let's start simple.

A language model is like a robot brain that's trained to understand and generate human language. It reads text and learns how words and sentences are typically put together.

Now, when we say "large" language model, we're not talking about its size on a scale or how much it eats!

We're talking about:

- How much data it has been trained on (think billions and billions of words), and

- How many "neurons" or "connections" it has (like a brain with LOTS of thinking power).

Think of a small language model as a toddler learning to speak and a large language model as a college professor who's read the entire internet!

How Did We Get Here? A Little History!

Let's rewind the clock a bit.

The Early Days

In the early 2000s, we had some smart programs that could predict the next word in a sentence. For example:

"The cat sat on the..."
It would guess "mat."

But those early models were limited. They could only think one or two words ahead. It was like trying to finish a sentence with your eyes closed.

Enter Neural Networks

Then came something awesome called neural networks — computer models inspired by how our brains work. They could recognize patterns and learn better over time.

In 2013, researchers developed a technique called word embeddings (think of them as map coordinates for words, so "king" and "queen" would be close). It helped machines understand meanings better, not just words.

2018: The "Transformer" Revolution

Here comes the superstar moment — the Transformer architecture (no, not the robots from movies.
Google introduced a model called BERT in 2018. Transformers allowed models to read entire paragraphs at once and understand the context of words — not just one by one but all together like a smart reader.

This was a game-changer. Suddenly, machines could understand jokes, write stories, and even answer questions like a pro.

What Made Large Models Possible?

Good question! Let's peek under the hood. Here's what helped LLMs rise to fame:

1. Massive Data

Think of the internet as the world's biggest library. Large language models are trained on tons of online text: books, news, Wikipedia, websites — even Reddit posts!

It's like feeding the AI a lifetime supply of reading material so it learns how humans talk, write, and even argue online.

2. Big Computers

Training these models needs supercomputers — not your regular laptops. They use special chips (called GPUs [Graphics Processing Unit] and TPUs [Tensor Processing Unit]) that process huge amounts of information very quickly.

Imagine training a language model is like teaching a million kids at once. You need a giant classroom with speakers, screens, and LOTS of power.

3. Smart Algorithms

We needed clever math tricks to make all this work. One of the coolest is "self-attention," where the model learns which words to focus on.

If I say:

"The animal didn't move. It was made of stone."

What does "it" mean here?
The model has to realize "it" refers to the animal, and "made of stone" means it's a statue, not a real creature.

So, What Can These Models Do?

Oh boy — a lot! Let's list some fun stuff:

- Write essays, poems, or stories (like a creative author)
- Chat with people (like a chatbot or tutor)
- Help scientists and doctors with research
- Draft emails, job posts, or resumes
- Explain topics like a teacher — from physics to painting
- Generate images when paired with tools like DALL·E

And yes — they can even write jokes. Sometimes bad ones.

Why Are They So Impressive?

Large language models can "understand" and "create" language almost like humans. Of course, they don't actually have feelings or consciousness — they don't think like we do — but they've learned the patterns of how we speak.

It's like they've read every book ever written, watched all the conversations, and then learned how to mimic human responses really well.

Imagine asking a magical parrot trained on the entire internet — that's sort of what it's like!

Where Do We Stand Now?

In 2020, OpenAI launched GPT-3, which became super popular. It could write poems, answer questions, even write code.
Then came ChatGPT, which turned GPT into a friendly chatbot anyone could use.

In 2022–2024, more advanced versions arrived — like GPT-4 — with better memory, reasoning, and even visual understanding.

Now, companies like Google (with Gemini), Anthropic (with Claude), and Meta (with LLaMA) have their own language models too. It's like a science fair of super-smart robots competing to help humans!

Fun Analogies to Help You Remember

- **Training a language model** is like teaching a parrot to talk by letting it read millions of books.
- **Using a model like ChatGPT** is like having a magical librarian who reads your question and instantly finds an answer in their mind.
- **Prompting** it is like typing a wish to a genie: the clearer you are, the better your wish turns out.

In Summary

- Large language models are super smart text machines trained on tons of data.
- They became powerful thanks to transformers, data, and computing power.
- They help us with writing, learning, researching, coding, and more.
- They're not perfect — they can make mistakes or be confusing — but they're learning fast.
- And they're changing how humans and machines interact. Big time.

So next time you chat with an AI like me, remember — you're talking to a giant brain that grew from millions of conversations, books, and ideas. And the way you talk to it (your prompt!) matters.

Why prompts matter

Hello again, brilliant minds!

Today, we're diving into a very important topic that might seem small at first... but trust me, it's mighty: Why prompts matter when talking to AI!

Think of prompts as the magic spell you cast to wake up your AI genie. If the spell (prompt) is vague, the genie gets confused. But if it's clear and specific, you get exactly what you wished for.

Let's explore this together — like a classroom adventure!

What Is a Prompt, Again?

In case you've just joined us, a prompt is the message, question, or instruction you give to an AI (like me!). It could be something simple like:

"Write a story about a dragon."

Or it could be something specific like:

"Write a funny bedtime story for kids under 8 about a shy purple dragon who's afraid of loud roars."

That's a prompt. It's how you talk to the AI.

Why Is the Prompt So Important?

Because AI doesn't read your mind (yet). It only understands what you write — and how you write it.

- If your prompt is too vague, the AI might not know what you want.
- If your prompt is too complicated, it might get confused.
- But if your prompt is clear, focused, and friendly, it's like giving the AI a perfect map to follow!

Here's why prompts truly matter:

1. **They Guide the AI Like a Compass**

Imagine the AI is a super-talented chef. But here's the thing: they're standing in a kitchen filled with every ingredient in the world.

Now you walk in and say:

"Make something tasty."

The chef goes: "Uhh... sushi? Pizza? Fruit salad?"

But what if you said:

"Make a vegetarian pasta with mushrooms and a garlic cream sauce."

Boom! Now the chef knows exactly what to make.

Your prompt is like that — it tells the AI where to go and what ingredients (words, tone, format) to use.

2. They Set the Style and Tone

Want your AI to sound like a pirate? A poet? A professor? A puppy? The way you write your prompt sets the personality of the response.

Example:

"Explain gravity."
You'll probably get a neutral, textbook-style answer.

But try this:
"Explain gravity to a 10-year-old using a trampoline and a bowling ball as examples."

Suddenly, it's a fun little physics lesson with metaphors!

Prompts matter because they control how the AI talks — not just what it says.

3. They Influence Creativity and Structure

Your prompt tells the AI how creative to be, how long to write, and what format to follow.

Let's say you want a poem:

Basic prompt: "Write a poem."
Result: Could be anything from a haiku to Shakespeare.

Better prompt: "Write a funny 4-line poem in rhyme about a cat who thinks it's a dog."

Now you're giving clear rules and a playful idea — and the AI responds accordingly.

You're the director, and your prompt is the script.

4. They Help the AI Understand Your Intent

Sometimes humans say things that sound clear to us, but not to a machine.

For example:

"Write an article on Mars."

Wait — Mars the planet?
Mars the chocolate brand?
Mars as in Roman mythology?

But if you say:

"Write a 300-word article for 6th-grade students about the planet Mars and its red appearance."

Now the AI understands your intent.

Prompts matter because they reduce misunderstandings.

5. They Help You Experiment

Prompts are fun to tweak! Like seasoning a dish — a little change brings a whole new flavour.

Try this:

"Tell a story about a robot learning emotions."

Then change it slightly:

"Tell a sad story about a robot learning emotions in a world without humans."

Totally different vibes, right?

Prompts give you creative control. You're experimenting with ideas, feelings, and outcomes — all through words.

6. They're Tools for Every Kind of User

Whether you're:

- A student writing an essay,
- A teacher explaining algebra,
- A marketer drafting ad copy,
- A coder asking for Python help, or
- A storyteller inventing a new world...

Your prompt is your starting point. A powerful one.

Good prompts = great results
Weak prompts = mixed or confusing results

The magic is in how you ask!

Quick Before & After Examples

Let's make it more fun! Here are some prompt upgrades:

Basic Prompt	Better Prompt
"Write about trees."	"Explain why trees are important to the environment using simple words for middle school students."
"Give a speech."	"Write a motivational speech for students who just failed an exam but want to try again."

Basic Prompt	Better Prompt
"Make a list."	"Make a list of 5 fun indoor activities for kids stuck at home on a rainy day."

See? It's like giving your AI helper a flashlight and a map instead of saying, "Figure it out yourself!"

Bonus Analogy Time!

Here are some fun metaphors to remember:

Prompt = Your wish to the genie

Prompt = The script for your actor

Prompt = The blueprint for your builder

Prompt = The target for your archer

Prompt = The compass for your explorer

Prompt = The spice in your AI dish

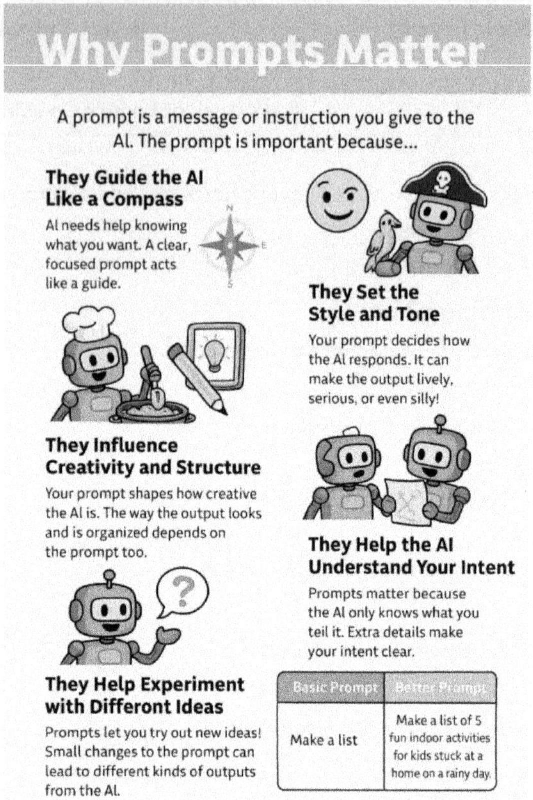

In Summary

Prompts are your way of “talking” to AI.

The clearer, more specific, and more thoughtful your prompt, the better the AI performs.

You control tone, style, detail, and structure.

Prompts are like programming, but with words instead of code.

With practice, you’ll master the art of guiding AI to do exactly what you want.

So next time you ask something, remember:
Prompts are not just questions. They're your superpower.

And you — yes, YOU — are the prompt wizard in charge.

Ready to start crafting some magical prompts? Let's keep learning!

From Programming to Prompting: The Big Shift in How We Talk to Machines

Hey there, curious minds!
Buckle up, because today we're going on a time-travel journey — from the world of traditional programming to the exciting new world of prompting!

This shift isn't just about how we interact with computers — it's about who can do it and how easy (and fun!) it has become. So, let's dive in, like a fun teacher would walk you through your first science experiment.

What Is Programming?

Let's start at the beginning.

Programming is how humans talk to computers — using special languages like Python, Java, or C++. It's like writing detailed recipes for a very literal robot chef:

Step 1: Turn on oven
Step 2: Chop onions
Step 3: Cry (optional)

You have to be very specific. If you mess up a semicolon or bracket, the whole thing breaks. Programming is powerful, but it's also picky.

To learn programming, you need to understand:

- Logic
- Syntax (special rules)
- Algorithms

- Sometimes math

That's why programming used to be a job mostly for... well, programmers!

And Now... Prompting!
Prompting is something magical that's come with the rise of large language models (LLMs) like ChatGPT.

Instead of telling the computer how to do something in code, you simply ask it in plain language — like you're talking to a very smart friend:

"Hey AI, write me a bedtime story about a panda who wants to fly."

That's it. No semicolons. No loops. No brackets.
And voilà! The AI writes the story.

This is prompting — giving natural-language instructions to a model that understands and generates human-like responses.

The Big Shift: Programming → Prompting

Let's break this down like a cool teacher would on the whiteboard:

Programming	Prompting
Uses code like for(i=0; i<5; i++)	Uses plain English like "repeat this 5 times"
Requires deep training	Accessible to anyone who can write
Very precise, but less flexible	More flexible, but needs clarity
Traditional way to build apps, games, websites	New way to interact with AI models

The Core Difference Between Programming & Prompting?

Programming tells a machine HOW to do something.
Prompting tells a model WHAT you want, and it figures out HOW.

Why Is This a Big Deal?

Because now anyone can do amazing things with technology — without writing a single line of code!

A few examples:

A teacher can say:

"Make a lesson plan for 4th-grade math with fun games."

A marketer can say:

"Write a product description for my eco-friendly water bottle."

A student can say:

"Explain the French Revolution in simple terms for a school report."

And the AI does it. Magic? No. Prompting!

This means:

Creativity is unlocked for more people.

Barriers to entry are lower — no need to spend years learning programming first.

Tech becomes conversational, not just computational.

But Wait! Is Prompting Replacing Programming?

Whoa there! Not exactly.

Prompting isn't killing programming — it's adding a new layer.

Think of it like this:

Programming is analogous to: Building the foundation (walls, pipes, wiring).
Prompting is analogous to: Decorating the house (paint, furniture, style).

So yes, AI developers still write complex code behind the scenes. But for users — you and me — we now have a smoother, friendlier way to interact with these smart tools.

Prompting and programming are partners, not rivals. One builds the engine, the other turns the key.

Prompting Is a New Literacy

In the 20th century, reading and writing were essential skills.
In the 21st century, prompting might become just as important!

Think about it:

Want a summary of a long article? Prompt it.

Need code for a calculator app? Prompt it.

Want an image of a frog wearing sunglasses? Prompt it.

Knowing how to ask — clearly, creatively, and effectively — is the new superpower.

Prompting in Action: Real Examples

Let's say you're trying to create a simple calculator using Python.

Programming version:

```
def add(a, b):
    return a + b
```

Prompting version:

"Give me a Python function that adds two numbers."

Boom! The AI gives you the same code.

Or maybe you're trying to write a poem.

If you write a prompt like:
"Write a 4-line funny poem about a chicken who wants to be an astronaut."

The AI writes the 4-line poem for you. You tweak it. No coding needed.

Why It Matters for the Future

Here's why the shift from programming to prompting is so revolutionary:

- **More people can create things** — apps, stories, designs, ideas.
- **Faster results** — what used to take hours in code can be done in minutes with a prompt.
- **Human language becomes the new interface** — no more needing to "speak computer."

It's the future of interaction:

- Conversational technology.
- Smart tools, human words.
- Powerful results.

But Prompting Still Takes Skill!

Just like good writing or public speaking, prompting is an art.

You'll still need to:

- Be clear and specific
- Add context and tone
- Try different versions to improve results

So, while it's easier than coding, it still rewards those who practice and experiment.

And guess what? That's you — right now!

Final Thought: From Programmers to Prompt-Masters

The world is changing — and that's a good thing.

You don't have to be a computer genius anymore to use powerful tools. You just need curiosity, creativity, and a little practice with prompts.

Whether you're a student, artist, writer, entrepreneur, or dreamer — prompting puts the power in your hands.

You're not just using technology now — you're collaborating with it.

And that, dear learner, is the heart of this new digital age.

End of Chapter Exercises – 1

1. In the passage, prompt engineering is described as "programming with words." What is the primary reason for this comparison?

   A) Because prompt engineering requires learning formal syntax like programming languages

   B) Because prompts, like code, are precise instructions that shape the machine's output

   C) Because prompt engineering uses special libraries similar to programming frameworks

   D) Because both prompts and programs can only be written in English

2. Which example best illustrates **user control through prompt engineering** as explained in the text?

   A) Asking "Tell me about cats" and receiving a general summary

   B) Saying "Explain this like a teacher" to influence style and tone

   C) Typing "Write about science" and expecting a poem

   D) Letting the AI generate random outputs without context

3. The analogy of asking a child to pack lunch highlights what core principle of prompt engineering?

   A) AI outputs are unpredictable no matter how specific you are

   B) Simplicity in prompts ensures the AI always guesses correctly

   C) Detailed instructions lead to results closer to the user's intent

   D) Children and AI both require identical training methods

4. According to the historical section, why were **Transformers (2018)** a turning point for large language models?

   A) They introduced symbolic reasoning that replaced neural networks

   B) They enabled models to process entire passages simultaneously for context

C) They reduced computing costs so small laptops could train models

D) They eliminated the need for training data altogether

5. In the "chef analogy" of prompts, why is "Make something tasty" considered ineffective?

   A) It forces the chef to ignore user intent completely

   B) It demonstrates that broad instructions leave too many possible interpretations

   C) It requires the chef to guess based on personal preference

   D) It proves that AI cannot handle creative tasks

6. Which of the following is **NOT** listed as a factor that enabled the rise of large language models?

   A) Smart algorithms like self-attention

   B) The use of GPUs and TPUs for faster computation

   C) Billions of words of internet-scale training data

   D) Advances in symbolic AI rule-based systems

7. What is the **key difference** between programming and prompting, according to the passage?

   A) Programming requires imagination, prompting requires logic

   B) Programming tells the machine HOW to do something, prompting tells WHAT is wanted

   C) Programming is conversational, prompting is computational

   D) Programming always produces creative outputs, prompting always produces factual outputs

8. Why does the passage call prompting a "new literacy" of the 21st century?

   A) Because it is harder to learn than coding

   B) Because everyone will need it to pass school exams

C) Because knowing how to ask AI effectively is becoming as essential as reading and writing

D) Because it will replace all human communication

9. In the "genie analogy" for prompting, what is implied if the user gives a vague prompt?

   A) The genie (AI) will refuse to answer until more details are provided

   B) The genie will misinterpret and provide unexpected or odd results

   C) The genie will always produce the same answer regardless of wording

   D) The genie gains more power and autonomy

10. Which summary BEST captures the passage's explanation of the partnership between programming and prompting?

    A) Prompting will soon eliminate the need for programmers

    B) Programming builds the foundation, prompting decorates and directs usage

    C) Prompting is strictly for creative writing, programming for technical work

    D) Prompting requires less creativity but more mathematical skill than programming.

End of Chapter Exercises – 2

1. A data analyst writes:

   "You are an expert in financial forecasting. Analyse the attached dataset for trends and outliers, and then generate a one-page report suitable for executives with graphs and plain-English summaries."

   Is this effective prompt engineering?
   a) Yes – it sets role, task, audience, and output format
   b) No – too vague for real-world use
   c) No – too complex, AI won't follow
   d) Yes – but only because it asks for graphs

2. A student writes:

   "Tell me about history."

   Is this effective prompt engineering?
   a) Yes – simple and clear
   b) No – overly broad, lacks scope, role, or detail
   c) Yes – AI can still handle it
   d) Yes – but depends on context

3. A UX designer asks:

   "List 5 innovative ideas for a meditation app. Rank them by novelty and feasibility. Output in a comparison table."

   Effective?
   a) Yes – structured request with ranking + table
   b) No – too many constraints
   c) No – doesn't define audience
   d) Yes – but only because it says "innovative"

4. A user writes:

   "Give me code."

   Effective?

   a) Yes – it will give code anyway
   b) No – lacks purpose, context, or language
   c) Yes – concise requests work
   d) Yes – but only for small snippets

5. A lawyer writes:

   "Explain GDPR Article 17 in 200 words, using examples relevant to social media companies, and make it easy for a non-lawyer to understand."

   Effective?

   a) Yes – clear scope, target audience, and constraints
   b) No – too limiting
   c) Yes – but examples reduce precision
   d) No – AI can't summarize law accurately

6. A travel blogger writes:

   "You are a sarcastic tour guide. Describe Paris in a funny, over-the-top way, focusing on food and romance. Write 3 short paragraphs."

   Effective?

   a) Yes – role + tone + style + constraints = strong prompt
   b) No – humour is too subjective
   c) Yes – but AI may fail on sarcasm
   d) No – not structured

7. A programmer writes:

   "Generate a Python function that sorts a list. That's it."

   Effective?

   a) Yes – simple and AI can do it
   b) No – lacks performance criteria or edge cases

c) Yes – minimalism is best practice

d) No – too vague to be useful in production

8. A doctor writes:

   "Summarize this patient's record and predict their future medical risks."

   Effective?

   a) Yes – clear request

   b) No – unsafe, requires medical expertise & real-world data caution

   c) Yes – AI can still help

   d) Yes – if anonymized

9. A teacher writes:

   "Design a 3-day lesson plan on renewable energy for 10-year-olds. Include activities, games, and quizzes. Present it as a bullet-point list."

   Effective?

   a) Yes – precise, structured, audience-specific

   b) No – too detailed for AI

   c) No – unclear output style

   d) Yes – but only if AI knows pedagogy

10. A marketing intern writes:

    "Write me something about AI that I can post on LinkedIn."

    Effective?

    a) Yes – short and flexible

    b) No – vague, lacks audience, tone, format, or length

    c) Yes – AI will fill the gaps

    d) Yes – but depends on creativity

3. How Generative AI Understands Prompts

(And What Happens Behind the Scenes!)

Hey there, curious explorer!

Have you ever typed something into an AI like ChatGPT and wondered, "How on earth did it understand what I meant?"

Today, we're going to open the AI's brain (not literally!) and see how it reads, thinks, and responds to your prompts. We'll explore this in three fun and fascinating parts:

1. Anatomy of a Language Model
2. Tokenization and Context Windows
3. Temperature, Top-p, and Other Parameters

Let's break it all down, teacher-style — like we're in a classroom where robots are the students!

Anatomy of a Language Model

Let's start with the big question:

What is a language model?

Well, imagine a giant brain that has read more books, articles, conversations, and websites than any human ever could. This brain is trained to do one magical thing: predict the next word.

Yes, really! That's the core of it.

Let's try a little exercise:

If I say: "The sun rises in the..."
What word pops into your head?

You probably said "east." That's because your brain knows the most likely next word.
AI does the same thing, but on a HUGE scale. It doesn't think or feel. It just predicts, using patterns.

How It Works (in simple terms)

When you give the AI a prompt like:

"Write a poem about the moon."

It doesn't know what a "moon" really is. But it's seen that word millions of times in its training and knows what usually comes next when people write about it.

So, word by word (or actually token by token — more on that next!), it builds a response like:

"The moon shines bright in silver light..."

It's like a super-powered autocomplete machine — one that doesn't just finish your sentences but writes full stories, songs, or explanations.

Tokenization and Context Windows

Now, let's open the next chapter of our AI anatomy lesson:

How does the model read your prompt?

This is where we meet two new friends:

1. Tokens
2. Context Windows

What Are Tokens?

Think of tokens like puzzle pieces. When you type something, the AI breaks it into chunks called tokens. These aren't always whole words!
For example:

"Beautiful" → might become one token, or could break into: "Beauti" + "ful" (2 tokens).
"Unbelievable" → could break into: "Un" + "believ" + "able" (3 tokens!)

This helps the AI understand even parts of words and weird spellings.

For reference, 1 token is roughly 3/4th of a word in English, so 100 tokens would typically mean 75 words in English.

Why does this matter? Because AI doesn't see sentences like we do. It sees streams of tokens, which are like the Lego blocks of language.

What's a Context Window?

Now imagine a window through which the AI looks at all those tokens. This window is called the context window, and it has a maximum size.

Think of it like this:

You're writing on a scroll.

The AI can only see the last few feet of that scroll — not the whole thing.

That "few feet" is your context window.

If your prompt (and the AI's response so far) fits in the window, great!
But if it's too long, the beginning starts sliding out of view like tape being pulled too far.

So, small models might have a window of 2,000 tokens.

Bigger models, like GPT-4-turbo & 4o can handle around 128,000 tokens, GPT-5 can handle around 200,000 tokens.

That's why longer prompts allow for better understanding — up to a point.
More tokens = more memory space = deeper context.

Temperature, Top-p, and Other Parameters

Now let's add some spice to this recipe!
How does the AI decide how creative, random, or safe its responses are?

That's where parameters come in. These are like dials and switches you can adjust when using AI. The most important ones are:

Temperature

Think of temperature like a creativity dial.

Low temperature (0 to 0.3) = Calm and focused.

"Just the facts, please."

High temperature (0.8 to 1.0) = Wacky and wild.

It changes how risky the model is with its word choices.

Example:

Prompt: "What's the capital of France?"

Temp 0: "Paris."

Temp 1.0: "The swirling city of croissants and dreams — Paris!"

Same question, different flavour.

Top-p (a.k.a. Nucleus Sampling)

If temperature is about how random the choices are, top-p is about which options are allowed.

It works like this:

The model predicts the next word and ranks options by probability.

Top-p = the percentage of total probability mass to consider.

So:

Top-p 1.0 = consider all possible words.

Top-p 0.9 = only use the top 90% of likely words.

Top-p 0.1 = use only the safest guesses.

Example:

If the top options for the next word are:

"apple" (40%), "banana" (30%), "cucumber" (20%), "dragon" (10%)

Then:

Top-p 0.9 = considers apple, banana, cucumber

Top-p 0.5 = might only allow "apple"

This makes responses more predictable or more fun — depending on what you want.

Other Parameters (just a peek!)

- **Max tokens:** Limits how long the AI's response can be.
- **Stop sequences:** Tells the AI where to stop generating.
- **Presence/frequency penalties:** Adjust how often it repeats itself.

Don't worry — most apps handle these behind the scenes.

But it's good to know they exist. Like training wheels on a bicycle, they help the AI ride smoothly without going off-road!

Wrapping It All Up

Let's recap what we learned today, shall we?

Topic	What You Learned
Anatomy of a model	Predicts next word based on patterns
Tokens	Words are broken into tiny chunks
Context window	Limited space for memory and attention
Temperature	Controls creativity and randomness
Top-p	Chooses which word options to consider
Parameters	Let us tweak how the model responds

So, when you type a prompt into ChatGPT or any generative AI, you're not just tossing words into a black hole. You're giving it instructions — and those instructions get tokenized, analysed, and sampled with creativity controls — all in milliseconds!

Isn't that amazing?

Teacher's Final Word

Prompts may look like just words on a screen. But under the hood? There's a world of math, logic, and language magic working together.

And the best part?
You don't need to be a programmer to use it. You just need curiosity — and the right words.

Now that you know how the AI understands you, you're ready to prompt like a pro!

How Generative AI Understands Prompts

Anatomy of a Language Model

Predicts the next word based on patterns in the text

Prompt: *"Write a poem about the moon."*

Response: *"The moon shines-bright in the sky..."*

Tokens

Breaks text! into smaller chunks

'Beautiful' → 'Unbelieva 'bi1be" ';able"

Context window

Context window

Maximum amount of text that a model can consider at once

Temperature, Top-p, and Other Parameters

Temperature: Controls creativity and randomness

Temperature

- **Low:** Just the facts, please."
- **High:** "Let's make it a poem *about* a pirate riding a unicorn!"

Top-p (a.k.a. nucleus sampling)

Chooses which word options

- **Top-p 1.0:** Considers all possibilities

Top-p 0.5: Considers only top 50%

End of Chapter Exercises

1. When an AI language model generates text, its core function is best described as:

   a) Understanding the semantic meaning of human intent

   b) Predicting the next token based on learned patterns

   c) Recalling memorized examples from training

   d) Translating user prompts into symbolic logic

2. Which of the following illustrates **why tokenization is essential** in AI processing?

   a) It makes the AI store full words for better memory

   b) It ensures the model only sees complete sentences

   c) It lets the AI remove unnecessary context

   d) It allows AI to process text in chunks smaller than or equal to words

3. Why does the **context window size** limit an AI's ability to respond to long prompts?

   a) Because tokens that fall outside the window are ignored during prediction

   b) Because AI cannot store any tokens beyond its maximum training length

   c) Because context windows force AI to compress information into smaller tokens

   d) Because larger context windows make AI responses less accurate

4. If a user sets **temperature = 0**, what outcome is most likely?

   a) The AI produces repetitive nonsense

   b) The AI generates highly imaginative content

   c) The AI outputs deterministic, fact-based responses

   d) The AI refuses to answer unpredictable prompts

5. In the example with **top-p nucleus sampling**, why would setting top-p = 0.5 restrict creativity?
   a) Because only tokens within the most probable 50% are considered
   b) Because AI randomly selects from all words regardless of likelihood
   c) Because top-p forces the model to repeat high-frequency tokens
   d) Because top-p ignores the context window

6. Which scenario best illustrates the difference between **temperature** and **top-p**?
   a) Temperature changes which tokens are visible; top-p decides the order
   b) Temperature adjusts randomness; top-p limits the probability pool
   c) Temperature controls response length; top-p controls repetition
   d) Temperature sets the maximum tokens; top-p selects the next word deterministically

7. Why is the statement *"AI understands what the moon really is"* incorrect?
   a) Because AI can only access its training set, not real-world facts
   b) Because AI cannot tokenize words like "moon"
   c) Because AI cannot represent concepts beyond mathematics
   d) Because AI doesn't understand; it recognizes statistical patterns of usage

8. What happens if a prompt + response exceeds the context window limit?
   a) The AI compresses earlier tokens automatically
   b) Tokens at the beginning fall out of scope and are forgotten
   c) The AI expands the context window by increasing max tokens
   d) The AI stops generating output completely

9. Why might **low temperature (e.g., 0.2)** combined with **high top-p (1.0)** still yield deterministic answers?

   a) Because low temperature strongly biases towards the highest-probability token

   b) Because top-p overrides temperature entirely

   c) Because context window cancels top-p variation

   d) Because tokenization prevents randomness at low scales

10. If a developer wants the AI to avoid repeating itself in long-form responses, which parameter is most relevant?

   a) Temperature

   b) Top-p

   c) Frequency or presence penalty

   d) Context window size

4. Types of Prompts and Their Purpose

Introduction: Why Learn About Prompt Types?

Imagine talking to a genie who can grant your wishes — but only if you ask the right way! That's how prompts work with AI. The type of prompt you give determines the kind of response you get. Just like asking a friend to help you cook versus asking them to write a poem — the style of asking matters.

Now let's explore the four main types of prompts and see them in action!

Instructional Prompts

These are direct, clear commands or instructions given to the AI.
You're basically saying: "Hey AI, go do this specific task!"

Purpose

To make the AI perform a task with clarity and precision.

Format

Usually imperative (command-style).

Examples

"Summarize this article in three bullet points."

"Translate this sentence into French."

"List 5 benefits of regular exercise."

"Write an email apologizing for missing a meeting."

Instructional Prompts are Best for:

1. Academic writing
2. Coding assistance

3. Email drafting
4. Quick facts and research summaries

Conversational Prompts

These simulate human-like, back-and-forth dialogues.
They're more like: "Hey, can we chat about something?"

Purpose

To hold a flowing, contextual conversation that feels natural.

Format

More casual, often with questions or follow-ups.

Examples

"What are your thoughts on space tourism?"

"How does quantum computing differ from classical computing?"

"Can we talk about the French Revolution like we're two students studying for a test?"

"Hmm, I'm not sure I understand that part — can you explain it again?"

Conversational Prompts are Best for:

1. Learning through conversation
2. Brainstorming
3. Practicing interviews
4. Philosophical or ethical discussions

Creative Prompts

These invite the AI to imagine, create, and innovate!
You're saying: "Let's build a world together!"

Purpose

To generate unique content like stories, poems, jokes, scripts, or even artwork.

Format

Open-ended and imaginative. Sometimes quirky, sometimes poetic!

Examples

"Write a bedtime story about a robot who dreams of becoming a chef."

"Compose a haiku about rainy days and lost love."

"Describe a utopian city floating in the clouds."

"Create a dialogue between a pirate and a penguin."

Creative Prompts are Best for:

1. Storytelling
2. Song and poem writing
3. Game design ideas
4. Character creation
5. World-building in fiction

Chain-of-Thought (CoT) Prompts & Step-by-Step Reasoning

This prompt type guides the AI to "think aloud."
You're saying: "Don't just give me the answer — show your work!"

Purpose

To solve complex problems using logical steps. Helps in tasks that need multi-step reasoning.

Format

Often starts with "Let's think step by step..." or "Explain your reasoning..."

Examples

"If a train travels 60 km in 1 hour and then 90 km in the next 1.5 hours, what's the average speed? Let's think step by step."

"Can you explain why the moon causes tides on Earth? Break it down."

"Which number comes next in the sequence: 2, 4, 8, 16...? Explain the pattern."

CoT Prompts are Best for:

1. Math and science problems
2. Logical puzzles
3. Decision-making processes
4. Teaching and tutoring

Final Thoughts: Why All This Matters

Different prompts = different results. Knowing the right kind of prompt to use helps you:

- Save time
- Get more accurate results
- Unlock the full creative and cognitive power of the AI

It's like choosing the right spell for the right effect — and YOU are the wizard!

End of Chapter Exercises

1. Which of the following **most clearly distinguishes instructional prompts** from the other three types?

   a) They are structured as direct commands with clear, precise tasks

   b) They simulate dialogues with natural follow-ups

   c) They are open-ended, leaving room for imagination

   d) They require the AI to show its reasoning step by step

2. A student says to the AI: *"Hmm, I don't get that. Could you explain it in simpler words like you're my classmate?"*
   Which prompt type is this?

   a) Instructional

   b) Creative

   c) Chain-of-Thought

   d) Conversational

3. Which of the following is a **misuse** of a creative prompt?

   a) "Write a bedtime story about a robot who dreams of becoming a chef."

   b) "List three benefits of eating fruits daily."

   c) "Compose a haiku about rainy days and lost love."

   d) "Describe a utopian city floating in the clouds."

4. Why might a **chain-of-thought prompt** be especially powerful for math or logic questions?

   a) It allows the AI to simulate human-style reasoning step by step

   b) It forces the AI to invent new facts rather than reuse patterns

   c) It makes the AI more creative in storytelling

   d) It reduces the token count required for long responses

5. A teacher wants the AI to act like a co-learner during a history study session, asking questions and clarifying doubts as if in a classroom dialogue. Which prompt type should they primarily use?

   a) Instructional

   b) Creative

   c) Conversational

   d) Chain-of-Thought

6. Which subtle feature separates **creative prompts** from **conversational prompts**?

   a) Creative prompts require logical breakdowns; conversational prompts don't

   b) Creative prompts always include commands; conversational prompts never do

   c) Creative prompts are fact-based; conversational prompts are not

   d) Creative prompts generate imaginative outputs, while conversational prompts simulate back-and-forth dialogue

7. Which of the following best matches a **chain-of-thought prompt** in action?

   a) "Summarize this article in three bullet points."

   b) "Explain why photosynthesis depends on sunlight. Let's think step by step."

   c) "Write a love poem from the perspective of the ocean."

   d) "Can we chat about how democracy has evolved?"

8. If someone wants the AI to generate **an apology email**, which prompt type would be most appropriate?

   a) Conversational

   b) Chain-of-Thought

c) Instructional

d) Creative

9. A writer uses AI to generate character backstories for a fantasy novel. Which category of prompt are they primarily engaging with?

   a) Creative

   b) Conversational

   c) Instructional

   d) Chain-of-Thought

10. Which of the following is the **most accurate generalization** about prompt types?

    a) Instructional prompts are casual, conversational prompts are formal, creative prompts are logical, chain-of-thought prompts are imaginative

    b) Instructional prompts drive precise tasks; conversational prompts enable dialogue; creative prompts spark imagination; chain-of-thought prompts enhance reasoning

    c) Instructional prompts are best for facts, conversational for logic, creative for storytelling, chain-of-thought for brainstorming

    d) Instructional prompts always outperform the others when accuracy is needed

Part II: Prompting with ChatGPT and Claude

5. Crafting Text Prompts for ChatGPT & Claude

Hello, curious learners! Today we'll explore how to craft powerful text prompts for ChatGPT, Claude, or other conversational AI. Think of prompts as your magic words that guide the AI to be just the companion you need. We'll dive into the following key areas:

1. Role Prompting & Persona Design
2. System vs. User vs. Assistant Messages
3. Improving Coherence, Creativity, and Factuality

Let's make this fun, clear, and hands-on-just like your favourite teacher leading a lively class!

1. Role Prompting & Persona Design

Imagine asking a robot to wear a costume and play a part. That's what role prompting does: it sets who the AI should pretend to be.

Why it matters: A clear role helps the AI adopt the right tone, knowledge level, and style.

How to do it: At the start of your prompt, tell the AI who it is and what it should focus on.

Examples

Teacher Persona

"You are a patient math teacher explaining fractions to a 5th grader. Use simple language and fun analogies."

The AI will explain (actual ChatGPT reply):

****

Absolutely! Let's dive into the wonderful world of fractions in a fun and easy way.

What is a Fraction?
A fraction is just a way to show parts of a whole.
Imagine you have a pizza. If you cut it into 4 equal slices, and eat 1 slice, you've eaten 1 out of 4 slices. That's written as:

1/4 (said as "one fourth" or "one quarter")

Parts of a Fraction
A fraction has two parts:

Top number → called the numerator
(It tells how many parts you have)

Bottom number → called the denominator
(It tells how many parts the whole is cut into)

So, in 1/4:

1 = the part you have (numerator)

4 = the total parts (denominator)

Fun Analogy: Chocolate Bar
Imagine you have a big chocolate bar with 8 squares.

If you eat 3 squares, you've eaten 3 out of 8 or 3/8.

Fractions in Real Life
Fractions are everywhere:

Sharing a cake

Telling time (Half an hour = 1/2 hour)

Measuring ingredients in cooking

Let's Practice Together
Let's say you cut a sandwich into 2 equal parts, and eat one part.

How much did you eat?
Answer: 1/2 (One-half)

Tip to Remember
If you cut something into more pieces, each piece is smaller.

So:

1/2 is bigger than 1/4
(because halves are bigger than fourths)

Quick Quiz (Just for fun!)
You have a pie cut into 6 pieces. You eat 2. What fraction did you eat?
Answer: 2/6

A chocolate bar is split into 3 pieces. You give 1 to your friend. What fraction did your friend get?
Answer: 1/3

Would you like to play a fraction game next? Or draw some pizzas together and color the slices?
****

Friendly Travel Guide
"You are a cheerful travel guide. Recommend a 3-day itinerary for Rome, focusing on hidden gems."

Expect an Answer Like:
****

IT Buongiorno, traveller! Welcome to Rome, the Eternal City! Most tourists rush to the Colosseum and Vatican — and while they're amazing, we're going to take you off the beaten path and into Rome's delightful hidden gems. Ready for an unforgettable 3-day Roman adventure? Let's go!

Day 1: Trastevere Treasures & Aventine Magic

Morning — Explore Trastevere
Wander the cobbled streets of Trastevere — a charming, artsy neighbourhood full of ivy-covered buildings and colourful homes.

Visit Santa Cecilia in Trastevere, a peaceful 9th-century basilica with stunning mosaics and underground crypts.

Grab a cappuccino and maritozzo (sweet cream bun) at Pasticceria Valzani (a true local favourite).

Lunch
Eat at Tonnarello or Da Enzo al 29 — both known for pasta perfection (try cacio e pepe or amatriciana!).

Afternoon — Aventine Hill Secrets
Head to Aventine Hill, one of Rome's legendary seven hills. Stop at:

Orange Garden (Giardino degli Aranci) — Peaceful park with sweeping city views.

The Keyhole of the Knights of Malta - Peek through and see a perfect view of St. Peter's Basilica framed by hedges!

Evening — Sunset & Strolling
Cross the Tiber Island and enjoy a magical riverside walk.

Have dinner at Osteria der Belli — homemade Sardinian cuisine and great wine.

Gelato stop: Günther Gelato — creative flavours made from fresh ingredients!

Day 2: Underground Rome & Hidden Art

Morning — Underground Adventures
Visit Basilica di San Clemente — a 12th-century church built over a 4th-century church built over a 1st-century pagan temple. It's like time travel underground!

Explore the Case Romane del Celio — ancient Roman homes beneath a modern monastery. Quiet, eerie, and full of frescoes!

Lunch
Try a Roman-style pizza al taglio (by the slice) at Pizzarium Bonci (a bit outside the center, but worth the trip!).

Afternoon — Hidden Art & Peaceful Corners
Visit the Doria Pamphilj Gallery — a private palace with dazzling artwork (Caravaggio! Velázquez!) and zero crowds.

Walk through the Jewish Ghetto, rich in history and full of charming alleys. Don't miss Fontana delle Tartarughe (Turtle Fountain).

Evening — Aperitivo & Local Vibes
Watch the sun set from Pincian Hill Terrace in Villa Borghese Gardens.

Dinner at Osteria dell'Ingegno — cozy, modern twist on Roman classics.

Evening walk through Piazza di Pietra — ancient columns lit up at night. So romantic!

Day 3: Quieter Vatican Corners & Markets

Morning — Vatican Without the Crowds
Instead of the main museums, visit Vatican Gardens (book in advance for guided tours) — peaceful, lush, and rarely visited.

Explore Santo Stefano degli Abissini, a tiny Ethiopian church inside the Vatican — almost always empty!

Lunch — Roman Market Style!
Visit Testaccio Market — a local food haven! Eat where the Romans eat. Try Trapizzino (stuffed pizza pockets!) or Mordi & Vai for delicious sandwiches.

Afternoon — Art & Cemetery (Yes, Really!)
Explore Centrale Montemartini — ancient statues in an old power plant! It's quirky and stunning.

Then visit the Non-Catholic Cemetery — peaceful, poetic, and the resting place of Keats and Shelley.

Evening — Celebrate Roman Style
Toast your trip with an aperitivo at Freni e Frizioni in Trastevere.

Final dinner at Roscioli — a Roman classic with world-famous carbonara.

End with a nighttime stroll by the Tiber River, lights reflecting like magic.

Bonus Tips:
Get lost on purpose — Rome's side streets are full of secrets.

Carry cash — some great local spots don't take cards.

Wear comfy shoes — the cobblestones are ancient (and wobbly!).

Are you ready to fall in love with Rome's quiet corners and hidden magic? Let me know if you want maps, restaurant bookings, or secret gelato codes.
****

Strict Editor

"You are a strict grammar editor. Improve this paragraph to be concise and professional: *You know what's seriously underrated? Just sitting outside on a slightly breezy evening with a good cup of coffee and no real plans. No meetings, no noise, just you, the sound of leaves rustling, and maybe a cat walking by like it owns the place. It's like the world hits pause for a second, and everything feels kind of okay — even if your to-do list is a mess. Moments like that don't fix everything, but man, they sure help."*

The AI will revise your text with precise corrections, like:

****

An often-overlooked pleasure is simply sitting outside on a breezy evening with a good cup of coffee and no obligations. No meetings, no noise-just you, the rustle of leaves, and perhaps a passing cat. It feels as though the world pauses briefly, offering a sense of calm even when life is chaotic. Such moments may not solve everything, but they offer quiet reassurance.

****

2. System vs. User vs. Assistant Messages

In ChatGPT's API and many AI platforms, messages are divided into three types:

Message Type	Who Writes It	Purpose
System	You (developer)	Sets overall rules, behavior, and context.
User	You (end-user)	Asks questions or gives tasks.
Assistant	AI model	Provides the AI's response.

How to Use Each

System Message

Establishes the AI's behavior for the entire session.

Example

System: "You are a helpful assistant. Always reply in under 100 words."
Result: AI will keep answers concise.

User Message

Contains your question or instruction.

Example

User: "Explain photosynthesis in simple terms."
The AI interprets this based on the system context.

Assistant Message
The AI's replies become part of the conversation history.

Helps maintain context for follow-ups.

Example

Assistant: "Photosynthesis is how plants turn sunlight into food. They use leaves like solar panels..."

Why It's Important
System messages keep the AI on track (tone, style, boundaries).

User messages are your real-time requests.

Assistant messages build memory—so the AI "remembers" what you talked about.

3. Improving Coherence, Creativity, and Factuality
Getting the right mix of clear, imaginative, and accurate responses often needs a few prompt-tuning tricks.

A. Coherence
Make your request logical and step-by-step.

Tip: Ask for outlines or numbered steps.

Example

"List the three main causes of World War I, then explain each in two sentences."
This encourages the AI to produce organized, on-point answers.

B. Creativity

To spark creativity, give open-ended cues and examples.

Tip: Use vivid descriptors and ask for unique angles.

Example

"Write a short fantasy story about a time-traveling cat. Include at least one humorous mishap."
The AI will feel free to invent playful scenarios.

C. Factuality

To guard against mistakes:

- Ask for sources or citations.

"Explain Newton's laws and cite one reliable source for each law."

- Request verification.

"List three facts about Mars. Then say, 'I am confident in these facts.'"

- Use temperature control.

Lower temperature (e.g. 0.2) makes answers conservative and fact-based.

Higher temperature (e.g. 0.8) increases creativity (but more risk of errors).

4. Putting It All Together: A Sample Prompt

System: "You are a friendly history tutor. Keep answers under 150 words."

User (Role & Instruction): "As a history teacher, explain the significance of the Renaissance. Use an engaging story style for high-school students." Parameters (Creativity/Factuality): "Use temperature 0.3 for accuracy. End with one suggested reading."

What Happens Next?

The system message ensures your tutor stays friendly and concise.

The role prompt ("As a history teacher...") guides tone and audience.

The temperature setting keeps facts reliable.

The AI will craft a short, engaging narrative about how the Renaissance revived art and learning, then suggest a book like "The Renaissance: A Short History."

Final Tips & Tricks

- Be explicit about tone, length, and style.
- Combine system messages with role prompts for best results.
- Experiment with parameters (temperature, top-p) to find your sweet spot.
- **Iterate:** If the first answer isn't perfect, tweak your prompt and try again!

With these strategies, you'll become a prompt-crafting wizard — guiding ChatGPT or Claude to produce content that's coherent, creative, and accurate.

Now go forth and prompt with confidence!

End of Chapter Exercises

1. Which statement best describes the purpose of role prompting & persona design?

a) To adjust AI parameters like temperature for factuality
b) To guarantee the AI never makes errors
c) To instruct the AI to adopt a specific tone, style, or knowledge level
d) To divide messages into system, user, and assistant types

2. You ask ChatGPT: *"You are a cheerful travel guide. Suggest a 3-day itinerary for Tokyo focusing on hidden gems."*

Which aspect of prompt engineering does this exemplify?
a) Role & persona prompting
b) System message design
c) Temperature tuning
d) Coherence improvement

3. In ChatGPT API, what is the primary purpose of a system message?

a) To ask a question to the AI
b) To define creativity parameters like top-p
c) To set session-wide behavior, rules, and tone
d) To provide step-by-step reasoning

4. Which of the following best illustrates a user message?

a) "You are a helpful assistant. Always respond in under 100 words."
b) "Photosynthesis is how plants turn sunlight into food."
c) "Explain photosynthesis in simple terms."
d) "Set temperature to 0.2 for accuracy."

5. Why might you include temperature = 0.2 in a prompt?

a) To make AI answers highly imaginative
b) To ensure factual, conservative responses

c) To assign a role or persona
d) To improve conversational flow

6. Which combination of techniques is most likely to improve coherence in AI responses?

a) Role prompting + creative storytelling
b) Numbered steps + outlines + explicit instructions
c) High temperature + top-p = 1.0
d) Casual conversational prompts

7. Which of these is a good example of combining role prompting and instructions?

a) “List three facts about Mars. Then say, ‘I am confident in these facts.’”
b) “You are a helpful assistant. Always respond concisely.”
c) “Explain Newton’s laws and cite one reliable source for each.”
d) “As a history teacher, explain the significance of the Renaissance to high-school students in an engaging story style.”

8. When is top-p (nucleus sampling) particularly useful?

a) To assign the AI a specific persona
b) To limit which probable words are considered for the next token
c) To format a system message
d) To guide step-by-step reasoning

9. Which of the following is not a direct way to improve factuality in AI responses?

a) Ask the AI to provide citations or sources
b) Use low temperature settings
c) Request step-by-step reasoning
d) Explicitly instruct the AI to verify facts

10. You want ChatGPT to be both engaging and concise while explaining a topic. Which strategy is best?

a) Use a role prompt + system message + temperature tuning

b) Only assign a high-temperature creative prompt

c) Only divide messages into system, user, and assistant types

d) Avoid giving explicit instructions to see what AI produces

6. Prompt Recipes: Solving Real Problems

Hello, problem-solvers!

Imagine AI as your kitchen's all-star chef. You don't just shout "cook!" — you hand over a recipe, step by step, so the result is delicious. In AI, "prompt recipes" are structured instructions that turn broad tasks into precise outcomes. Today, we'll cook up four practical prompt recipes:

1. Summarizing Large Texts
2. Generating Emails & Reports
3. Coding Help & Debugging
4. Decision-Making with Pros & Cons

Let's grab our aprons and dive in!

1. Summarizing Large Texts

Why It Matters

Long articles, reports, or books can feel like a mountain to climb. A good summary saves time and highlights key points.

Prompt Recipe

This Prompt Recipe comprises of 3 things:

- **Instruction(s):** It is something like, "Summarize the following text..."
- **Scope:** Is where you specify length or some other parameter to limit the output ("in 5 sentences" or "bullet points").
- **Focus:** You need to ask for themes, outcomes, or action items.

Example

Prompt:

"Summarize this 2,000-word article on climate change in 5 bullet points, focusing on causes, impacts, and solutions."

AI Response Might Be:

****

1. Rising greenhouse gases from fossil fuels drive global warming.

2. Melting ice and sea-level rise threaten coastal cities.

3. Extreme weather events (storms, droughts) are increasing.

4. Renewable energy and reforestation can reduce emissions.

5. Global cooperation and policy changes are crucial.

****

2. Generating Emails & Reports

Why It Matters

Writing clear emails or reports takes time and thought. AI can draft a strong first version for you to tweak.

Prompt Recipe

This Prompt Recipe comprises of 3 things:

- **Role & Tone:** "You are a friendly project manager."
- **Purpose:** "Write an email to update stakeholders on progress."
- **Details:** Include project name, status, next steps, and thanks.

Example: Email

Prompt:

"You're a friendly project manager. Write an email to the "Green Park Renovation" team with:

A brief progress update (50% complete)

Upcoming tasks next week

Appreciation for the crew's hard work."

AI Response Might Be:

****

Subject: Green Park Renovation – Mid-Project Update
Hi Team,
I hope you're all doing well! We're 50% complete on the Green Park Renovation. The new pathways are laid, and planting begins next Monday.
Next Week's Tasks:

Install benches along the north lawn

Begin planting flower beds by the entrance

Test the irrigation system
Thank you for your hard work and dedication. Let's keep up the great momentum!
Best,
[Your Name]

****

Example: Report

Prompt:

"Write a one-page report on Q2 sales performance: highlight total sales, top products, challenges, and recommendations."

AI will structure headings, metrics, and clear advice — almost like a template you can copy into Word.

3. Coding Help & Debugging

Why It Matters

Even seasoned coders get stuck on errors or need snippets fast. AI can suggest code or point out bugs.

Prompt Recipe

This Prompt Recipe can be a combination of any of the following (depends on what you want from AI):

Context: "Here's my code..."

Error: "I get this error message..."

Goal: "I want it to do X."

Example: Snippet Generation

Prompt:

"Write a Python function that reads a CSV file and returns a list of dictionaries, where each dictionary is a row keyed by header names."

AI Response Would be:

****

```
import csv

def read_csv_to_dicts(file_path):
  with open(file_path, newline='') as csvfile:
    reader = csv.DictReader(csvfile)
    return [row for row in reader]
```

****

Example: Debugging

Prompt:

"I have this JavaScript code:

```
function add(a, b) {
 return a + b;
}
console.log(add('2', 3));
```

It outputs "23" instead of 5. What's wrong and how to fix it?"

AI Explanation Would be:

****

Problem: '2' is a string, so '2' + 3 concatenates.

Fix: Convert to number: return Number(a) + b;

Or ensure inputs are numbers before calling.

****

4. Decision-Making with Pros & Cons

Why It Matters

Big or small choices — like picking a laptop or planning an event-benefit from organized pros and cons.

Prompt Recipe

- **Decision:** "Help me decide between A and B."
- **Criteria:** "Consider cost, performance, and ease of use."
- **Format:** "List pros and cons for each, then give a brief recommendation."

Example

Prompt:

"Help me decide between buying a MacBook Air or a Windows Ultrabook. Consider cost, performance, and portability. Provide pros and cons for each and recommend one."

AI Response Might Be:

****

MacBook Air
Pros:

Sleek design and lightweight (1.2 kg)

Excellent battery life (up to 15 hours)

Integrated Apple ecosystem
Cons:

Higher cost (starting at $999)

Limited port variety (only USB-C)

Windows Ultrabook
Pros:

Wider range of prices (from $700)

More ports (USB-A, HDMI)

Customizable hardware
Cons:

Battery life varies (8–12 hours)

Build quality depends on brand

Recommendation:
For portability and battery life, choose the MacBook Air. If budget and ports matter more, go for a Windows Ultrabook.
****

Final Serving Tips

- Be specific about length, format, and focus.
- Include roles (teacher, manager, coder) to set tone.
- Ask for lists or sections to keep answers organized.
- **Iterate:** If the first result isn't perfect, tweak your prompt and try again.

With these prompt recipes, you'll turn AI into your go-to helper for studying, writing, coding, and decision-making. Bon appétit!

End of Chapter Exercises

1. When summarizing a large text using a prompt recipe, which instruction ensures the AI focuses on actionable outcomes rather than general statements?

   a) "Summarize this article in one sentence."
   b) "Summarize this article randomly."
   c) "Summarize this article in 5 bullet points focusing on causes, impacts, and solutions."
   d) "Write a poem about this article."

2. In generating emails, why is including a **role and tone** in the prompt critical?

   a) It adds unnecessary complexity
   b) It forces the AI to include emojis
   c) It makes the AI ignore the content of the email
   d) It determines how the AI should format and phrase its response

3. Which of the following is the **best way to prompt AI for debugging code**?

   a) "Write random code for me."
   b) "Explain why code is bad."
   c) "I get this error message: ... Here's my code. I want it to do X."
   d) "Fix my code."

4. When creating a prompt for **decision-making with pros and cons**, which element is unnecessary?

   a) Randomly including unrelated information
   b) Listing criteria for evaluation
   c) Providing the options to compare
   d) Asking for a brief recommendation

5. What is the main advantage of specifying **length and format** when summarizing large texts or generating reports?

   a) It prevents the AI from generating long, unstructured responses
   b) It makes the AI output more creative
   c) It forces the AI to ignore key points
   d) It allows the AI to generate jokes

6. If you want an AI to generate a **friendly, detailed email update** for a project team, which of the following prompt components is most important?

   a) Temperature = 1.0
   b) Leave role unspecified
   c) Include project name, status, next steps, and thanks
   d) Ask the AI to improvise without context

7. When asking AI to write code that reads a CSV file, why is specifying the **expected output format** crucial?

   a) It ensures the output is structured exactly as needed (e.g., list of dictionaries keyed by headers)
   b) The AI will guess randomly
   c) It limits the AI's creativity
   d) It slows down processing

8. In the MacBook Air vs. Windows Ultrabook example, what makes the AI's recommendation reliable?

   a) It randomly chooses one option
   b) It considers **criteria, pros/cons, and provides a recommendation**
   c) It writes a long essay without structure
   d) It only lists pros and ignores cons

9. What is the purpose of iterating on a first AI response when using prompt recipes?

    a) To confuse the AI
    b) To improve the prompt and refine the output
    c) To change the AI model
    d) To increase the randomness (temperature) unnecessarily

10. Which strategy ensures AI generates both **coherent and creative content** in one prompt?

    a) Ask for random content with no instructions
    b) Leave all parameters at default without guidance
    c) Specify structure (steps, sections) and allow some creativity with role or tone
    d) Only provide system messages without role

7. Advanced Techniques

Hello, prompt pioneers!

You've mastered the basics, and now it's time to level up. In this lesson, we'll explore three advanced prompting techniques that unlock even more power from ChatGPT, Claude, or any large language model:

1. Few-Shot and Zero-Shot Prompting
2. Self-Reflection & "Think Step-by-Step"
3. Iterative Refinement & Meta-Prompts

Ready to supercharge your AI chat skills? Let's dive in!

1. Few-Shot and Zero-Shot Prompting

Zero-Shot Prompting

What it is: You ask the model to perform a task without any examples.

When to use it: The task is straightforward or you want a quick test.

Example (Zero-Shot)

Prompt:

"Translate this sentence into Spanish: 'The cat climbed the tree.'"

AI Response Would be

"El gato trepó al árbol."

Few-Shot Prompting

What it is: You provide a few examples in the prompt so the model sees the pattern.

When to use it: The task is tricky or you want the AI to follow a specific format.

Example (Few-Shot)

Prompt:

"Here are three English-to-Spanish translations:

Hello → Hola
Thank you → Gracias
Good night → Buenas noches
Now translate: 'The cat climbed the tree.'"

AI Response Would be

"El gato trepó al árbol."

Why It Helps: Few-shot examples act like mini-lessons. The AI picks up the style, tone, and structure you want.

2. Self-Reflection & "Think Step-by-Step"

"Think Step-by-Step"

What it is: You ask the AI to show its work, breaking down its reasoning.

Why it matters: Helps catch mistakes, improves accuracy, and makes the AI's thought process clear.

Example

Prompt:

"What is 17 × 24? Please think step-by-step."

AI Response Might Be:

****

Sure! Let's break down 17 × 24 step-by-step using simple multiplication techniques.

Step 1: Break one number into parts
Let's break 24 into 20 + 4

So:
17 × 24 becomes

👉 17 × (20 + 4)

✅ Step 2: Use distributive property
Now multiply 17 with both parts:

17 × 20 = ?
17 × 2 = 34 → Add one zero → 340

17 × 4 = ?
10 × 4 = 40
7 × 4 = 28
40 + 28 = 68

✅ Step 3: Add the two results
Now add:

340 + 68 = ?
340 + 60 = 400
400 + 8 = 408

🎉 Final Answer:
17 × 24 = 408 ✅
****

Self-Reflection

What it is: The AI reviews its own answer for possible errors or gaps.

How to prompt: Ask it to check or critique its previous reply.

Example

Prompt:
"Explain why the sky is blue, then reflect on your explanation and point out any uncertainties."

AI Response Would be:

****

Sure! Let's first explain why the sky is blue, and then take a step back to reflect on the explanation and its possible uncertainties.

🌤 Why is the Sky Blue?
The sky appears blue because of a phenomenon called Rayleigh scattering.

Here's how it works, step by step:

Sunlight looks white, but it's actually made up of many colors — red, orange, yellow, green, blue, indigo, and violet — which together form the visible spectrum.

When sunlight enters Earth's atmosphere, it hits gas molecules (mainly nitrogen and oxygen).

These tiny molecules scatter the shorter wavelengths (blue and violet) much more than the longer ones (like red and yellow).

Even though violet light scatters more than blue, our eyes are more sensitive to blue, and some violet is absorbed by the upper atmosphere, so we see the sky as blue during the day.

🤔 **Reflecting on the Explanation**
While the explanation above covers the basics, let's consider some uncertainties or simplifications:

◆ **Human eye sensitivity:** The role of the eye's response to different wavelengths (like why we don't see violet strongly) is a bit simplified. The cones in our eyes respond differently to red, green, and blue light — and this affects how we "perceive" the sky's color.

◆ **Violet absorption:** It's often stated that violet is absorbed by the ozone layer, but this isn't always consistently explained or quantified. Some scientists argue that eye sensitivity plays a bigger role than ozone absorption.

◆ **Edge cases:** The sky isn't always blue. During sunrise and sunset, light travels through more atmosphere, and blue light is mostly scattered away — so we see reds and oranges. Also, on other planets with different atmospheres, the sky can be entirely different colors (like red on Mars!).

In Summary
The sky looks blue mainly due to Rayleigh scattering of sunlight in the atmosphere, with our human eyes favouring blue over violet. But the exact "shade" and cause involve a mix of physics, human biology, and even atmospheric chemistry — showing how nature often blends science in beautifully complex ways!
****

Why It Helps: Because Self-Reflection encourages the AI to self-audit, increasing trustworthiness.

3. Iterative Refinement & Meta-Prompts

Iterative Refinement

What it is: You tweak the prompt or ask for improvements in rounds.

Process

1. Write an initial prompt.
2. Review the response.
3. Adjust the prompt (add detail, clarify tone, correct errors).
4. Repeat until satisfied.

Example

Prompt 1:
"Write a business summary for our sales data."

Response 1: Too short, missing details.

Prompt 2:
"Write a detailed 200-word business summary of Q1 sales, including growth rate, top products, and market challenges."

Response 2: Better! You now have the details you need.

Meta-Prompts

What it is: You ask the AI to guide you in crafting or improving prompts.

Why use it: The AI helps you become a better prompt writer.

Example

Prompt: "Act as a prompt coach. Here's my prompt: 'Explain blockchain.' Suggest three ways to improve it for clarity and depth."

AI Response Would be:

****

Great — you're on the right track by keeping your prompt simple and direct! But to get a clearer and deeper answer from an AI (like ChatGPT or Claude), it helps to guide the response more intentionally. Here are three improvements you can make:

🔗 **1. Add a Target Audience**
Tell the AI who the explanation is for. This helps adjust tone, vocabulary, and depth.

Original: "Explain blockchain."
Improved:

"Explain blockchain to a high school student using simple analogies."

"Explain blockchain to a tech-savvy entrepreneur who's new to crypto."

🔗 **2. Specify the Purpose or Focus**
"Blockchain" is a broad topic. Do you want history, how it works, use cases, pros/cons?

Improved Prompts:

"Explain how blockchain works, including how blocks are added and secured."

"Give an overview of blockchain with a focus on real-world business applications."

"Explain the benefits and risks of using blockchain in finance."

🔗 **3. Ask for a Format**
This helps structure the answer. Depending on what you need (a summary, step-by-step, comparison), you'll get better clarity.

Improved Prompt:

"Explain blockchain in a step-by-step format with examples."

"Compare blockchain to a traditional database, highlighting key differences."

"Explain blockchain as a story or analogy involving a group of friends passing notes."

✅ **Final Example Prompt:**
"Explain blockchain to a high school student using simple analogies and a step-by-step format. Focus on how data is stored securely and why it's considered trustworthy."

Would you like me to help rewrite your prompt based on your actual goal or audience?
****

Wrapping Up

By using few-shot and zero-shot methods, asking the AI to think step-by-step, conducting self-reflection, and refining your prompts iteratively (or with meta-prompts), you'll produce clearer, more accurate, and highly tailored outputs.

Practice these techniques, mix and match them, and watch your AI collaborations soar!

End of Chapter Exercises

1. What is the key difference between zero-shot and few-shot prompting?

   a) Zero-shot requires no examples; few-shot includes a few examples to guide the AI.
   b) Zero-shot provides multiple examples; few-shot provides none.
   c) Zero-shot uses random examples; few-shot uses templates.
   d) Zero-shot is only for translation tasks; few-shot is for coding tasks.

2. Why might few-shot prompting be preferred over zero-shot for a complex task?

   a) It makes the task simpler than intended.
   b) It prevents errors completely.
   c) It reduces the AI's response time.
   d) It shows the AI a pattern or style to follow.

3. In "Think Step-by-Step" prompting, what is the primary benefit?

   a) It shows the AI's reasoning in detail, catching errors and improving accuracy.
   b) It allows the AI to generate jokes along the way.
   c) It makes the AI produce fewer words.
   d) It ensures the AI guesses the answer randomly.

4. Self-reflection in AI prompting primarily helps with:

   a) Increasing response creativity only.
   b) Reviewing its own answer to identify gaps or uncertainties.
   c) Reducing computational cost.
   d) Making responses shorter.

5. Which of the following best describes iterative refinement?

   a) Only using zero-shot prompts repeatedly.
   b) Writing multiple prompts randomly without checking responses.

c) Tweaking the prompt in rounds based on previous responses to improve clarity and detail.

d) Giving one prompt and accepting the first response.

6. What is the purpose of a meta-prompt?

   a) To generate random responses.

   b) To avoid specifying a role for the AI.

   c) To trick the AI into giving faster answers.

   d) To let the AI help you improve your own prompts for clarity and depth.

7. Why is including a target audience in a prompt important?

   a) It ensures the AI ignores formatting.

   b) It restricts the AI from completing the task.

   c) It adjusts tone, vocabulary, and depth according to the audience.

   d) It reduces creativity by half.

8. When would zero-shot prompting be most appropriate?

   a) When the task is very complicated and requires many examples.

   b) When you want a quick answer for a straightforward task.

   c) When you want the AI to perform self-reflection.

   d) When you need iterative refinement.

9. Which is a correct example of iterative refinement in practice?

   a) Only giving examples in a few-shot prompt.

   b) Asking the AI to "Explain blockchain" once and accepting the response.

   c) Asking the AI to generate a poem instead.

   d) Gradually adding details, clarifying tone, and adjusting focus in repeated prompts.

10. What is the advantage of combining few-shot prompting with “think step-by-step” instructions?

    a) It reduces creativity significantly.

    b) It encourages structured reasoning while following a desired pattern or format.

    c) It guarantees the AI will never make mistakes.

    d) It only works for language translation tasks.

Part III: Prompting Visual and Multimodal Models

8. Prompting DALL·E and Image Generators

Let's dive into the magical world of prompting DALL·E and image generators. Imagine you're holding a paintbrush, but instead of dipping it in colors, you dip it in words! You describe a scene, a style, or a character, and — poof! — the AI paints it for you. But to get what you really want, you need to master the art of the prompt. So, let's break it down into our three exciting subtopics:

1. Crafting Visual Descriptions

Think of this as writing a script for a movie scene — but you're describing it to someone who can't see, only imagine.

What's the goal?

To clearly explain what you want the image to contain, from objects to scenes to actions.

How to do it?

Be specific. Don't say "a man with a hat"; say "an old man wearing a wide-brimmed cowboy hat, leaning on a wooden fence at sunset."

Use concrete nouns and vivid adjectives. They paint mental pictures.

Include action if needed. "A cat playing a violin" is much more interesting than "a cat."

Example Prompts

A dragon

"Create a very colourful and vibrant image of a fire-breathing red dragon with golden horns, flying over a medieval village at dusk."

AI Response Would be

****

****

A beach

"Create an image of a tropical beach with turquoise waters, palm trees, and a hammock swaying in the breeze."

AI Response Would be

****

****

2. Controlling Style, Color, Emotion, Realism

This is where the personality of the image comes alive. Think of it like choosing the mood, wardrobe, and lighting for a photoshoot!

What's the goal?

To guide the AI in terms of how the image should look and feel.

How to do it?

Mention art styles. Like watercolour, cyberpunk, anime, renaissance painting, pixel art.

Specify mood or emotion. "Melancholic," "joyful," "mysterious."

Control realism. Use terms like hyper-realistic, photorealistic, cartoon-style, surreal.

Color palette. Add "in pastel tones," "dark and moody lighting," or "vibrant neon colors."

Example Prompts

Prompt:

"Create a colourful and vibrant image of a cozy mountain cabin in winter, in watercolour style, with warm yellow lights glowing inside."

AI Response Would be

****

****

Prompt:

"Create a colourful and vibrant image of a futuristic cityscape in cyberpunk style, filled with neon lights and flying cars."

AI Response Would be

****

****

Prompt:

"Create a colourful and vibrant image of a photorealistic portrait of a smiling elderly woman with silver hair and kind eyes."

AI Response Would be

****

****

3. Common Issues and How to Fix Them

Even when you're doing everything right, DALL·E or other generators might throw you a visual curveball!

What could go wrong?

Weird limbs or distorted anatomy

Unclear subject focus

Wrong number of objects or people

Unwanted style/artifacts

How to fix it?

- Clarify the subject. Use words like "in focus," "central figure," or "main character."
- Set the scene order. Say "in the background," "to the left," or "in the foreground."
- Limit complexity. AI struggles with too many elements. Break it down or simplify.
- Use negative prompts (if supported). Add: "no text, no distortions, clear face."

Iterative tweaking

Sometimes you'll have to generate a few versions and refine the prompt each time. For example:

Initial Prompt: "A man riding a tiger under the moonlight"
Result: Man might look weird
****

****

Improved Prompt: "A brave warrior in detailed armor riding a majestic Bengal tiger under a full moon, photorealistic, centred, no distortions"
Result: Much better!
****

****

Bonus Tip: Combine it All!

Here's a magical master prompt combining everything:

"A fantasy castle floating in the sky, surrounded by soft clouds, in anime style. The castle is glowing with blue magical light. A princess in a flowing lavender gown stands at the balcony. Dreamy, soft lighting, pastel color palette, highly detailed."

****

****

Boom! Now you're not just prompting — you're directing a visual symphony.

So next time you think, "I wish I could draw this idea...", remember: with the right prompt, you already can! Just describe it like a storyteller, tune the style like a designer, and fix issues like a pro.

End of Chapter Exercises

1. What is the main purpose of crafting visual descriptions when prompting an image generator?
   a) To reduce the AI's processing time
   b) To enforce a specific file format for the output
   c) To limit the AI to using only one color
   d) To clearly explain what objects, scenes, or actions should appear in the image

2. Which of the following is an example of a detailed visual description for a dragon?
   a) A dragon
   b) A red dragon
   c) A fire-breathing red dragon with golden horns, flying over a medieval village at dusk
   d) A cartoon dragon

3. How can you control the style, emotion, and realism of a generated image?
   a) By using zero-shot prompting
   b) By specifying art styles, mood, lighting, color palette, and realism
   c) By giving fewer examples to the AI
   d) By providing only the object names

4. Which of the following would help fix unwanted distortions or unclear subjects in an AI-generated image?
   a) Add more characters to the scene
   b) Use negative prompts, clarify the subject, set scene order, and limit complexity
   c) Avoid giving any details in the prompt

d) Only request black-and-white images

5. What does the term "iterative tweaking" refer to in image generation?

   a) Generating multiple versions and refining the prompt based on results

   b) Using a single prompt repeatedly without changes

   c) Asking the AI to think step-by-step

   d) Creating prompts without specifying style

6. Why is including actions in your visual description important?

   a) It allows the AI to skip background details

   b) It makes the image prompt shorter

   c) It makes the image more dynamic and interesting

   d) It restricts the AI to photorealism

7. Which is an example of controlling the color palette in a prompt?

   a) "A dragon"

   b) "A tropical beach with turquoise waters, palm trees, and a hammock swaying in the breeze"

   c) "A fantasy castle floating in the sky, surrounded by soft clouds, dreamy, pastel color palette"

   d) "A cityscape"

8. Why is specificity important when prompting DALL·E or similar image generators?

   a) It reduces the file size of generated images

   b) It prevents the AI from generating multiple images

   c) It ensures only cartoon-style images are produced

   d) It guides the AI to produce the intended scene, characters, and details

9. Which of the following best describes a “master prompt” strategy?
   a) Give minimal instructions to let the AI improvise
   b) Combine detailed description, style, lighting, color palette, and character placement into one prompt
   c) Use zero-shot prompts exclusively
   d) Focus only on the background objects

10. How can negative prompts improve AI-generated images?
    a) By randomly changing the color palette
    b) By requesting multiple copies of the image
    c) By instructing the AI what to avoid, e.g., “no text, no distortions, clear face”
    d) By shortening the description to one word

9. Multimodal Prompting

Let's deep dive into the colourful, fascinating, and super-useful world of Multimodal Prompting — and don't worry, I'll be your energetic, story-telling, fun-loving teacher for this ride.

Multimodal Prompting: refers to supercharging Creativity with Text, Images & Audio.

Imagine you're a master chef. Your ingredients? Text, images, and audio. Separately, they're great — but together, they make a Michelin-star masterpiece!

That's what multimodal prompting is all about: blending different modes of input to make prompts richer, more expressive, and better suited to complex tasks.

Let's explore it through our two key subtopics:

1. Combining Text, Image, and Audio Prompts

Multimodal prompting allows you to combine different types of inputs — not just boring old text, but also images and even audio. This creates layered, context-rich interactions with AI models like GPT-4o, Gemini, and Claude.

Let me break it down like a fun science experiment:

Text + Image

Let's say you upload an image of a medieval castle and write:

Prompt: "Describe this scene in the style of a fantasy novel prologue."

Now the AI sees the castle and reads your instruction. It may respond with:

"The towering stone walls stood defiant against centuries of storms. Beneath the blood-red sky, whispers of forgotten magic lingered in the ivy-strewn halls..."

Pretty cool, right? The text gives instruction, and the image adds context. Together, they paint a richer picture.

Text + Audio

Let's say you upload a voice note of someone speaking emotionally and say:

Prompt: "Summarize what this speaker is feeling and what topic they are discussing."

Boom! The AI can analyse tone, pace, pitch, and word content to give you a nuanced emotional and contextual summary, which can be great for:

- Customer support calls
- Podcast planning
- Therapy session transcriptions

Text + Image + Audio

This is the Avengers Assemble moment.

Let's say you're creating a virtual art museum app. You upload:

- An image of a sculpture
- Audio of a visitor describing their thoughts
- And this text:

  "Analyse the sculpture's design and tell me how viewers emotionally respond to it."

Now, you're asking the AI to look, listen, and read to give a smart, multi-angle response, which is perfect for:

- Interactive learning
- Museum guides
- AI-assisted content curation

2. Use Cases: Presentations, Marketing, and Content Creation

Let's apply all this awesome tech to real-world scenarios!

A. Presentations That Pop

Gone are the days of dry PowerPoints. Want to create slides that actually wow?

Use Multimodal Prompting to:

- Upload a company logo
- Record your rough verbal explanation of your pitch
- Add a text prompt like:

  "Turn this into a clean, persuasive investor slide deck with visual themes matching the uploaded logo."

Now you're not just prompting a slide maker — you're building a co-creator.

Bonus: Want image suggestions? Just add:

"Give each slide a background image suggestion to support the message."

B. Marketing Magic

Marketing is about emotion, vibe, and visual + verbal coherence. Let's say you're launching a beachwear brand.

You upload:

- An image of a sun-soaked beach
- Prompt:

  "Create three Instagram captions with emojis. Each one should match the beach vibe and target young adults."

Want more flavour? Add a mood board and voice memo:

- Mood Board of pastel tones
- Voice note saying: "Keep it breezy, Gen-Z, and slightly cheeky."

Now the AI has vibe data, voice, and visual context to nail your branding.

C. Content Creation Superpowers

Let's say you're a teacher creating an e-learning video.

Use multimodal prompting to:

- Upload a concept map
- Include a sample lecture audio
- Add prompt:

  "Create a storyboard for a 5-minute animated explainer. Include visuals, key narration, and mood tone."

Suddenly, your AI is your co-teacher! It's reading your flow, sensing your tone, and crafting content that feels right.

Summary: Why Multimodal Prompting is the Future

Mode	Adds Value
Text	Instruction, logic, structure
Image	Visual context, emotion, scene
Audio	Tone, mood, natural speech, emotion

Mixing them is like using all the senses. And when your AI sees, hears, and reads — it understands more deeply and performs better.

Final Tip from Your Friendly AI Teacher

Start simple:

"Here's an image. Write a haiku."

Then level up:

"Here's an image, a voice memo, and a brief. Create a pitch, then summarize it in three tone variants."

Soon, you'll be an AI whisperer — conjuring results like a wizard.

End of Chapter Exercises

1. What is the primary advantage of multimodal prompting over traditional text-only prompts?

   a) Faster AI processing

   b) It reduces memory usage

   c) It limits AI creativity

   d) AI can understand complex tasks using multiple inputs like text, images, and audio

2. In the example of Text + Image prompting, what does the image contribute?

   a) It gives instructions to the AI

   b) It serves as a context-rich visual for the AI to describe

   c) It generates audio output

   d) It determines the file format of the AI response

3. How does Text + Audio prompting enhance AI understanding?

   a) By increasing text length

   b) By analysing tone, pitch, and pace to infer emotion and context

   c) By generating images automatically

   d) By limiting AI output to bullet points

4. Which scenario exemplifies the full multimodal approach (Text + Image + Audio)?

   a) Uploading a single photo for a caption

   b) Writing a paragraph with only text instructions

   c) Uploading an image of a sculpture, an audio commentary, and a textual prompt asking for analysis

   d) Using text to ask the AI for weather data

5. Why is multimodal prompting particularly useful for presentations?

   a) It shortens the AI's response time

   b) It ensures slides are only in black-and-white

   c) It eliminates the need for human input entirely

   d) It allows AI to integrate logos, voice explanations, and text prompts to create slides that match visual themes

6. In marketing applications, what does combining a mood board, text prompt, and voice note allow the AI to do?

   a) Translate content into multiple languages

   b) Capture vibe, tone, and visual context to produce coherent branding material

   c) Generate background music automatically

   d) Limit creativity to predefined templates

7. How can a teacher use multimodal prompting for content creation?

   a) Upload a concept map, lecture audio, and text prompt to generate a storyboard for an animated explainer

   b) Only use text to describe slides

   c) Convert the audio into a PDF

   d) Generate random multiple-choice questions without context

8. According to the summary table, what unique value does audio input provide in multimodal prompting?

   a) Instruction and logic

   b) Visual scene and context

   c) Tone, mood, natural speech, and emotion

   d) Formatting and text length

9. Which of the following best represents a beginner-friendly multimodal prompt?
   a) Upload multiple images, a voice memo, and a long text brief
   b) "Here's an image. Write a haiku."
   c) "Analyse this dataset in Excel and generate a report."
   d) "Write a detailed essay with no input."

10. What is the ultimate benefit of mixing text, images, and audio in AI prompts?
   a) Reduces AI training requirements
   b) Ensures the AI only produces textual outputs
   c) Provides all-senses input so AI understands more deeply and produces richer results
   d) Limits AI to one specific task per prompt

10. Prompting Other Tools: Midjourney, Stable Diffusion, Runway

Let's go full deep-dive mode with the energy of a fun, curious teacher who's had one too many coffees but is determined to make this lesson a blast! Buckle up — we're talking about the wonderful world of prompting other creative AI tools like Midjourney, Stable Diffusion, and Runway. These are powerhouse image and video generation platforms — but they only shine when you learn to "talk" to them well.

Let's break this topic down into three core subtopics:

1. Style-Based Prompts

Alright students, imagine walking into an art gallery. You can say:
"Paint me a dog."

And boom — every artist gives you a totally different version! Van Gogh gives you a swirling sky pup, Picasso tosses in cubes and triangles, while a hyperrealist paints every hair follicle. That's exactly how AI works with style-based prompting.

What are Style-Based Prompts?

Style-based prompts are text inputs where you not only describe the subject, but also define the artistic direction you want — such as the era, medium, lighting, mood, or artist inspiration.

How Do You Use Them?

To get the best results, always follow this golden format:

[Subject], in the style of **[Art form/Artist/Medium]**, **[Mood or Lighting]**, **[Environment or Detail]**

Examples

Prompt:

"A mystical forest fox, in the style of Studio Ghibli, warm light, fantasy background" – Midjourney will swoon.

****

****

Prompt:

"A futuristic Tokyo alleyway, cyberpunk aesthetic, rain-soaked neon lights, ultra-realistic style" – Stable Diffusion will snap that out like a sci-fi dream."

****

****

Prompt:

"An elegant ballerina dancing in moonlight, painted like Monet, soft brushstrokes, pastel palette" – Now Runway's visuals will make your jaw drop.

****

****

Why It Matters?

Each tool responds differently to style indicators.

Midjourney loves poetic, expressive language and picks up well on moods and references like "Baroque" or "vintage photography."

Stable Diffusion is more literal — it needs clear structure and benefits from technical terms like "ISO 100, 50mm lens, f/1.8."

Runway, especially with Gen-2, handles both style and motion cues. So, you could say, "Dreamlike transition from desert to rainforest, cinematic, smooth camera pan" for a video.

2. Fine-Tuning vs. Natural Prompting

Let's go professor mode here 🎓, because this is critical thinking time.

What's Fine-Tuning?

Fine-tuning is when you train the model on a specific style, face, or theme using custom datasets. You're not just prompting anymore — you're teaching the model what "your version" of art looks like.

For example: An animation studio wants to maintain a consistent visual across scenes. They train the model on their past art to create that style.

And Natural Prompting?

That's our everyday usage. You type a prompt, and the model guesses what you want based on pre-learned data.

"A wizard in a steampunk laboratory" - The tool paints based on general internet-trained data.

Comparing Both

Aspect	Fine-Tuning	Natural Prompting
Customization	High – can match your unique style	Limited – based on model's training
Effort	Requires data prep + training time	Just type and go
Cost	Can be resource-intensive	Usually free or built-in
Use Case	Brand identities, film production	Casual art, experimentation

Tools That Support This

1. **Runway** lets you train models on your footage or photos.
2. **Stable Diffusion (via DreamBooth)** supports fine-tuning for personal avatars or themes.
3. **Midjourney** doesn't allow custom model training but lets you build "custom styles" through prompt tricks and consistent references.

Example

Without fine-tuning:

"A girl with a golden crown, oil painting style"

****

****

Results vary per generation.

With fine-tuning:

"Create a hyper-realistic image of an elderly woman as shown in the attached image in royal dress" — in Stable Diffusion, you can achieve character consistency by clicking on image to image and uploading a reference image.

Result = same elderly woman, same vibe, every time. Consistency would be almost 100%.

I uploaded the below depicted image:

And the result is as shown below:

****

****

3. Prompt Libraries and Tools

Okay, think of prompt libraries as your AI prompt cookbooks. You don't always have to invent a recipe from scratch. Sometimes, the secret sauce is already written — you just need to spice it up!

What Are Prompt Libraries?

Prompt libraries are collections of effective, tested prompts that creators share. They help you avoid the trial-and-error dance.

Useful Tools and Sites

1. **PromptHero:** It is like a Pinterest for prompts — especially great for Midjourney and Stable Diffusion.
2. **Lexica.art:** It shows you prompts along with the generated images from Stable Diffusion. Fantastic for visual reverse engineering.
3. **Krea.ai:** It offers prompt tweaking, inspiration, and image-based feedback.
4. **Runway's Prompt Presets:** This is especially helpful in Gen-2 video generation — gives creative inspiration for transitions, themes, etc.

How to Use Them Smartly?

You don't copy-paste blindly! Use them as templates. Swap out subjects, tweak moods, or insert your own ideas.

Examples

From PromptHero, you can get a prompt like:

"Cyberpunk city, rainy, neon lights, bustling crowd, photorealistic"

You can adapt this into:

"Cyberpunk cafe interior, cozy neon glow, anime characters sipping tea, cinematic angle"

From Lexica, you can get a prompt like:

"Portrait of a samurai, dramatic lighting, brushwork style of Rembrandt"

Tweak it into:

"Female samurai warrior, storm in background, chiaroscuro lighting, style of Caravaggio"

Bonus Tip

Midjourney users often chain styles like:

"Portrait of a woman, 8k, ultra-detailed, trending on ArtStation, octane render, dark academia fashion, symmetrical lighting"
The results? Chef's kiss!

Final Thoughts: Prompting Like a Pro

Midjourney, Stable Diffusion, and Runway are like incredibly skilled artists. But their brilliance depends on how well you guide them. Think of prompts like instructions to a magician — the clearer and more vivid your imagination, the more stunning the spell they cast.

Use style cues. Learn the strengths of each tool. Fine-tune when you need consistency. Explore prompt libraries to get inspired. And above all, play, experiment, remix, and create. These tools are your playground — go have fun!

Let's wrap this session with a class mantra:

"Describe with clarity, imagine with creativity, prompt with purpose!"

End of Chapter Exercises

1. Which factor is most critical in style-based prompting for AI tools like Midjourney, Stable Diffusion, and Runway?

   a) Prompt length

   b) Subject description, artistic style, mood/lighting, and environment details

   c) Using only single-word prompts

   d) Limiting prompts to pre-existing datasets

2. How does Midjourney primarily respond to prompts compared to Stable Diffusion?

   a) Midjourney requires technical camera settings like ISO and f-stop

   b) Midjourney thrives on poetic and expressive language, while Stable Diffusion benefits from structured, technical terms

   c) Both treat prompts identically

   d) Midjourney ignores mood or lighting

3. Which of the following is a correct golden format for a style-based prompt?

   a) [Subject], [Single Word]

   b) [Art Style], [Color Palette], [Subject]

   c) [Mood], [Lighting], [Subject]

   d) [Subject], in the style of [Art form/Artist/Medium], [Mood or Lighting], [Environment or Detail]

4. What is the main advantage of fine-tuning over natural prompting?

   a) Reduces cost

   b) Generates casual art faster

   c) High customization and consistent style replication

d) Eliminates the need for text prompts

5. Which tool does NOT currently allow custom model training for fine-tuning?
   a) Runway
   b) Stable Diffusion
   c) Midjourney
   d) DreamBooth

6. Prompt libraries are useful because they:
   a) Contain pre-tested prompts that save trial-and-error time
   b) Replace the need for human creativity
   c) Force AI to output only text
   d) Restrict AI to one style per prompt

7. Which platform is highlighted for its prompt presets specifically aiding **video generation**?
   a) Stable Diffusion
   b) Midjourney
   c) Runway Gen-2
   d) Lexica.art

8. What is the purpose of tweaking prompts from libraries like PromptHero or Lexica?
   a) To copy content verbatim
   b) To avoid using AI tools
   c) To adapt subjects, moods, and styles for new creative outputs
   d) To prevent AI from generating images

9. Which combination best represents a high-quality style-based prompt for Stable Diffusion?

   a) “A dog”

   b) “A dog in Studio Ghibli style, with ISO 100, 50mm lens, f/1.8, warm lighting, forest background”

   c) “Dog, forest, cute”

   d) “Just generate an image”

10. Which mantra best summarizes expert prompting for creative AI tools?

    a) “Type fast, generate random, repeat”

    b) “Limit creativity, reduce input, restrict AI”

    c) “Always fine-tune, never experiment”

    d) “Describe with clarity, imagine with creativity, prompt with purpose”

Part IV: Use Cases and Domains

11. Prompting for Business

Prompting isn't just for techies and AI nerds anymore - it's your new business partner, working 24/7, never asking for coffee breaks. Whether you're running a startup, working in a marketing firm, or a freelancer building a personal brand, knowing how to prompt the right way can unlock a goldmine of productivity.

This topic is divided into three power-packed subtopics:

1. Copywriting, branding, SEO
2. Market research and competitive analysis
3. Automating repetitive tasks

1. Copywriting, Branding, and SEO – Prompting Your Way to a Magnetic Identity

Let's begin with the core of marketing: copywriting, branding, and SEO.

A. Copywriting

At its heart, copywriting is storytelling with a purpose. You want to sell something, right? Be it a service, a product, or even an idea — good copy is what grabs attention, holds it, and converts it.

With prompting, you can:

1. Generate headline options for your blog or ad campaigns.
2. Create persuasive product descriptions.
3. Write different versions of CTAs (Call-to-Actions).

Example Prompt

"Write 5 compelling product descriptions for a luxury vegan leather handbag, targeting millennial women who care about sustainability."

AI Output Would Be

****

Here are 5 compelling product descriptions for a luxury vegan leather handbag, written to resonate with millennial women who care about sustainability:

1. The Conscious Chic Companion
Step into timeless elegance without compromise. Crafted from premium vegan leather, this handbag brings together sleek design and eco-responsible craftsmanship. Perfect for your morning coffee runs, evening brunches, and late-night plans-it's as versatile as your lifestyle. Carry your essentials in style while carrying your values with pride.

2. Luxury, Reimagined for the Planet
Why choose between fashion and ethics when you can have both? This luxury vegan leather handbag is soft to the touch yet resilient, made with cruelty-free materials that last. Designed for the modern woman who believes sustainability is the new luxury, it turns every outfit into a statement of both beauty and responsibility.

3. Effortless Elegance Meets Everyday Utility
From boardroom to weekend getaway, this handbag was designed with you in mind. Thoughtfully engineered compartments keep your essentials organized while the sleek silhouette complements every outfit. Made with high-quality vegan leather, it proves that functionality and eco-conscious luxury can walk hand in hand.

4. A Handbag That Tells Your Story
This isn't just an accessory — it's a reflection of your values. With its minimalist design and ethical construction, this vegan leather handbag speaks volumes without saying a word. Durable, stylish, and consciously made, it lets you embrace sophistication while staying true to what matters most: compassion and sustainability.

5. Where Style Meets Sustainability

Turn heads for all the right reasons. This handbag, crafted from luxe vegan leather, radiates elegance while protecting the planet. Lightweight yet durable, it's the perfect companion for the woman who lives boldly, travels consciously, and refuses to compromise her style-or her ethics.

****

You can now refine it, adjust tone (e.g., formal, quirky, playful), and even generate multiple versions for A/B testing.

B. Branding

A strong brand voice is consistent, recognizable, and relatable.

With prompting, you can:

1. Craft your brand mission and vision statements.
2. Develop brand voice guidelines.
3. Create a value proposition that differentiates you.

Example Prompt

"Write a friendly yet confident brand voice guideline for a tech startup that creates smart home devices for senior citizens."

AI Output Would be

****

Here's a friendly yet confident brand voice guideline tailored for your smart home tech startup that creates devices for senior citizens:

🌟 Brand Voice Guidelines for [Your Startup Name]

Making Smart Homes, Simply Human.

1. Our Personality

We are warm, trustworthy, and empowering. Think of us as a caring family member who's also a reliable problem-solver. We want seniors to feel safe and confident, and their loved ones to feel reassured and connected.

Friendly: We explain technology as if we're chatting over tea.
Confident: We know what we're doing and we make life easier without overwhelming people with jargon.

Respectful: We never talk down to seniors. We value their independence and dignity.

Supportive: We provide encouragement, not pressure.

2. Tone of Voice

Our tone should always strike a balance between kindness and expertise.

Warm & Caring: "We're here to make your day a little easier."

Clear & Reassuring: "One button, and your lights adjust automatically. No hassle, no confusion."

Confident but Gentle: "Our devices are built with your safety in mind, and they're always reliable."

❌ Avoid being overly technical or patronizing.
✅ Use everyday language, relatable examples, and a positive outlook.

3. Vocabulary Guide
Words We Love:

Simple

Safe

Reliable

Connected

Comfort

Peace of mind

Independence

Words to Avoid:

Complicated tech jargon (e.g., "IoT ecosystems," "cloud-based protocols")

Infantilizing terms (e.g., "cute little gadget," "easy for old folks")

Overly aggressive salesy words (e.g., "must-buy," "limited time only")

4. Messaging Examples
Product Page:

Before: "This smart sensor uses advanced algorithms to detect activity in real-time."

After: "This smart sensor gently keeps an eye on your home, so you always know your loved ones are safe."

Customer Support:

Before: "Please reboot your device and reconnect it to the Wi-Fi router."

After: "Let's try a quick restart together. Press and hold this button, and your device will reconnect to Wi-Fi on its own."

Social Media:

Before: "Upgrade your smart home with our cutting-edge solutions!"

After: "Imagine your home adjusting the lights, checking doors, and keeping you cozy — all without you lifting a finger."

5. Voice in Action

Website Tagline: "Smart homes that care for you."

App Notification: "Good evening! Your doors are locked, and your home is secure."

Onboarding Email: "Welcome to a simpler, safer way of living. We're here with you every step of the way."

✨ **In short:** Our brand voice is a blend of friendliness and quiet confidence — like a tech-savvy friend who always has your back, without ever making you feel small.
****

C. SEO (Search Engine Optimization)

Prompting helps you:

1. Find target keywords.
2. Create meta descriptions, alt tags, and SEO-friendly titles.
3. Generate content outlines based on high-volume search terms.

Example Prompt

"Give me a list of long-tail keywords related to 'budget travel in Southeast Asia' and suggest blog titles that rank well on Google."

AI Output Would be

****

Got it 👍 You want long-tail keywords around "budget travel in Southeast Asia" + SEO-friendly blog title suggestions that could rank well. I'll break this into two parts:

🔍 Long-Tail Keyword Ideas for "Budget Travel in Southeast Asia"

These are specific, low-competition phrases people are actually searching for:

budget backpacking routes in Southeast Asia

cheapest countries to travel in Southeast Asia for backpackers

2 week budget travel itinerary Southeast Asia

cost of food and accommodation in Southeast Asia for travellers

budget travel tips for solo travellers in Southeast Asia

Southeast Asia on $30 a day travel guide

best budget hostels and guesthouses in Southeast Asia

cheapest ways to travel between countries in Southeast Asia

hidden gems in Southeast Asia for budget travellers

how to travel Southeast Asia long term on a budget

budget travel safety tips in Southeast Asia

best street food in Southeast Asia on a budget

budget-friendly island hopping in Thailand, Philippines, and Indonesia

visa costs and border crossings for budget travellers in Southeast Asia

ultimate Southeast Asia budget travel packing list

affordable eco-friendly travel in Southeast Asia

cheapest cities in Southeast Asia for digital nomads

how much does it cost to backpack Southeast Asia for 1 month budget alternatives to luxury destinations in Southeast Asia

travel mistakes to avoid in Southeast Asia on a budget

📝 Blog Title Suggestions That Rank Well

(Using click-worthy, SEO-friendly formats)

"Southeast Asia on $30 a Day: A Complete Budget Travel Guide"

"Cheapest Countries in Southeast Asia to Visit in 2025 (Backpacker's Guide)"

"2 Weeks in Southeast Asia: Budget-Friendly Itinerary for First-Timers"

"Ultimate Guide to Budget Travel in Southeast Asia for Solo Travelers"

"Backpacking Southeast Asia: How I Travelled for Under $1,000 a Month"

"Top 10 Hidden Gems in Southeast Asia for Budget Travelers"

"The Best Budget Hostels and Guesthouses in Southeast Asia"

"Island Hopping in Southeast Asia: Affordable Routes and Tips"

"Street Food Adventures: Eating Cheap and Delicious in Southeast Asia"

"Visa Costs, Border Crossings, and Travel Hacks for Southeast Asia on a Budget"

"The Ultimate Packing List for Southeast Asia Budget Travelers"

"Best Affordable Destinations in Southeast Asia for 2025"

👉 Pro Tip:

For SEO ranking, mix how-to guides + listicles + personal experience posts. Example:

"How I Travelled Southeast Asia for 3 Months on a $1,500 Budget"

"25 Budget Travel Tips Every Backpacker Needs in Southeast Asia"
****

2. Market Research and Competitive Analysis – Prompt Like a Business Detective

You don't need a private investigator to know what your competition is up to — just prompt smartly!

A. Market Research

Prompting helps with:

1. Generating customer personas.
2. Finding trends in customer behavior.
3. Analysing industry forecasts and challenges.

Example Prompt

"Generate three detailed customer personas for an online language learning app aimed at working professionals in Europe."

AI Output Would be

****

Perfect 👌 Let's create three rich customer personas tailored for an online language learning app for working professionals in Europe. I'll give each persona a name, demographics, goals, challenges, behaviors, and how the app fits their needs.

👩 Persona 1: Sophie Müller — The Career Climber

- Age: 29
- Location: Berlin, Germany
- Profession: Marketing Manager at a tech startup

- Languages: Native German, intermediate English, wants to learn Spanish
- Tech Habits: Heavy mobile user; uses apps like Duolingo, Notion, and Slack daily
- Income: €55,000/year

Goals & Motivations

- Wants to expand career opportunities in Spanish-speaking markets.
- Needs Spanish for client presentations and networking at international conferences.
- Aims to gain confidence in professional communication.

Challenges

- Works long hours, so struggles to find time for regular classes.
- Has tried free apps but found them too gamified and not practical for work-related vocabulary.
- Loses motivation without measurable progress.

Behaviors

- Studies best during short breaks or commutes.
- Prefers structured learning paths with clear milestones.
- Likes progress tracking and professional vocabulary modules.

How the App Fits

- Provides 10–15 min bite-sized lessons she can do at lunch or while commuting.
- Career-focused vocabulary packs (e.g., marketing, sales, presentations).
- Progress dashboard + certificates to showcase on LinkedIn.

👨 Persona 2: Marco Rossi — The Frequent Business Traveler

- Age: 41
- Location: Milan, Italy
- Profession: Senior Sales Executive at an international logistics company

- Languages: Native Italian, fluent English, learning French for clients
- Tech Habits: Uses laptop and phone interchangeably; values apps that sync across devices
- Income: €85,000/year

Goals & Motivations

- Wants to strengthen relationships with French-speaking clients.
- Needs conversational fluency for meetings, dinners, and negotiations.
- Seeks practical, business-oriented lessons rather than academic grammar.

Challenges

- Travels frequently, so cannot commit to scheduled classes.
- Feels self-conscious speaking a new language in formal settings.
- Finds generic apps too slow or irrelevant for his work.

Behaviors

- Learns during airport waits or hotel stays.
- Prefers audio-based lessons he can listen to while traveling.
- Responds well to roleplay simulations of real business scenarios.

How the App Fits

- Downloadable offline lessons for planes/trains.
- Business French conversation roleplays (e.g., negotiation, client dinners).
- Speech recognition + feedback to boost confidence.

👩🏾‍🦱 Persona 3: Clara Dubois — The Lifelong Learner

- Age: 35
- Location: Lyon, France
- Profession: Project Manager at an NGO
- Languages: Native French, conversational Spanish, wants to improve English for international collaborations
- Tech Habits: Active on LinkedIn and Coursera; loves structured e-learning experiences

- Income: €45,000/year

Goals & Motivations

- Wants to communicate effectively with colleagues across Europe and Africa.
- Needs professional English for reports, presentations, and Zoom calls.
- Motivated by personal growth as much as career advancement.

Challenges

- Sometimes lacks confidence speaking with native English speakers.
- Finds casual apps too simplistic; prefers serious, structured learning.
- Struggles with advanced grammar and business writing.

Behaviors

- Dedicates 30 minutes in the evening for study.
- Looks for community-based features (discussion boards, peer practice).
- Responds to clear learning paths with measurable achievements.

How the App Fits

- Offers business English modules (emails, project management, formal writing).
- Provides live conversation sessions with tutors for fluency practice.
- Includes peer learning groups for motivation and accountability.

✨ With these three personas — Sophie (career-driven), Marco (business traveller), and Clara (lifelong learner) — you cover the key segments of working professionals in Europe who need flexible, career-oriented, and practical language learning solutions.

****

B. Competitive Analysis

Use prompting to:

1. Compare your business with competitors.
2. Identify gaps or white spaces in offerings.
3. Draft SWOT (Strengths, Weaknesses, Opportunities, Threats) analysis.

Example Prompt

"Create a SWOT analysis comparing our eco-friendly shoe brand to Allbirds."

AI Output Would Be

****

Got it ☑ Let's do a SWOT analysis of your eco-friendly shoe brand compared to Allbirds. I'll structure it as a side-by-side comparison so you can clearly see where your brand might stand out or fall short.

🔘 **SWOT Analysis: Your Eco-Friendly Shoe Brand vs. Allbirds**

Category	Your Eco-Friendly Shoe Brand	Allbirds
Strengths	- Niche positioning: ability to tell a fresh sustainability story (materials, supply chain, local sourcing) - Agile and flexible: faster at innovating and testing new designs - Potential to target specific markets (e.g., Europe-only, luxury eco segment, or budget eco segment) - Can differentiate with **local identity** (e.g., "Made in Italy/Portugal") vs. Allbirds' global brand	- Global recognition as a sustainability leader - Strong brand loyalty & storytelling ("world's most comfortable shoe" + eco materials) - Wide product range: sneakers, running shoes, apparel - Retail presence in major global cities (US, Europe, Asia) - Proven track record of scaling eco-friendly production
Weaknesses	- Limited brand awareness compared to Allbirds - Smaller marketing budget and reach	- Criticism of being "mainstream" and less unique than before - Higher prices can alienate

Category	Your Eco-Friendly Shoe Brand	Allbirds
	- Potentially higher per-unit costs without economies of scale - Fewer SKUs and styles may limit customer choices	budget-conscious eco-shoppers - Some backlash over product durability (shoes wear out quickly) - Supply chain is global → higher carbon footprint despite eco focus
Opportunities	- Capitalize on growing **demand for sustainable fashion** in Europe (eco-conscious millennials, Gen Z) - Expand into **underserved niches**: affordable eco-shoes, luxury sustainable footwear, or workwear-friendly eco shoes - Leverage **direct-to-consumer digital marketing** to tell an authentic, local story - Collaborations with local artists, eco NGOs, or sustainable influencers	- Continue expanding beyond shoes into **eco lifestyle brand** (apparel, accessories) - Tap into growing **Asia-Pacific eco-fashion market** - Potential partnerships with global retailers (e.g., Nordstrom, Zalando) - Use its scale to invest in **R&D for new materials**
Threats	- Competition not only from Allbirds but also Veja, Cariuma, Adidas' sustainable lines, Nike's Move to Zero - Consumer skepticism: "greenwashing" concerns	- Newer indie eco-brands undercutting Allbirds on price & freshness - Luxury fashion houses launching sustainable collections (competition for eco-premium buyers)

Category	Your Eco-Friendly Shoe Brand	Allbirds
	in fashion - Rising costs of sustainable materials may shrink margins - Need to constantly educate consumers about eco-benefits	- Changing consumer perception: comfort/sustainability no longer unique differentiators - Increasing regulation on sustainability claims (EU Green Claims Directive)

Key Takeaways

- Your Brand's Advantage: Authenticity, agility, niche positioning (you can be more personal, community-driven, or regionally unique than Allbirds).
- Allbirds' Advantage: Global brand power, recognition, distribution, and product variety.
- Strategic Focus for You:

1. Double down on local authenticity (e.g., European craftsmanship, short supply chain).
2. Choose a clear niche (luxury eco, budget eco, or workplace eco shoes) instead of competing head-on in the general "eco sneaker" space.
3. Tell a fresh sustainability story that goes beyond what Allbirds already does (materials + social impact + durability).

****

In less than a coffee break, you've got solid data to guide your strategy.

3. Automating Repetitive Tasks – Prompting as Your Digital Assistant

Time is money. Automating repetitive tasks with prompting not only saves time but also increases consistency and accuracy.

A. Email Templates

Instead of writing every email from scratch:

Prompt AI to create cold email templates, follow-ups, thank-you notes, and client onboarding messages.

Example Prompt

"Write a warm but professional email follow-up to a lead who showed interest in our CRM software but hasn't responded in 5 days."

AI Output Would be

****

Here's a warm yet professional follow-up email you can send to your lead:

Subject: Just checking in - any thoughts on [Your CRM Software Name]?

Hi [First Name],

I hope this message finds you well. I just wanted to follow up since we last connected about [Your CRM Software Name]. I completely understand how busy things can get, but I thought I'd reach out to see if you had any questions or needed more information to evaluate whether our CRM might be a good fit for your team.

Many of our clients in [industry/role, e.g., mid-sized sales teams] have found that our platform helps them [insert key benefit, e.g., "save time on manual data entry and get clearer visibility into their pipeline"]. I'd be happy to walk you through a quick demo tailored to your use case or share a short case study if that's helpful.

Would you like me to schedule a quick 15-minute call later this week? If now isn't the right time, no worries at all — I'll be glad to reconnect whenever it suits you.

Looking forward to hearing from you.

Warm regards,
[Your Full Name]
[Your Position]
[Company Name]
[Contact Info]
****

B. Reports & Summaries

Prompting helps you:

1. Summarize meeting transcripts, interview notes, or survey feedback.
2. Auto-generate weekly reports.

Example Prompt

'Summarize this customer feedback: "Great quality, met my expectations.", "User-friendly and easy to set up.", "Value for money, worth it.", "Design is sleek and modern.", "Customer support was very helpful.", "Performance is fast and reliable.", "Could improve battery life.", "Packaging was eco-friendly and neat.", "Durable and feels premium.", "Would definitely recommend to others.". Group feedback into themes and suggest improvement areas.'

AI Output Would be

****

Here's a structured summary of the customer feedback grouped into themes, with improvement suggestions:

🌟 Positive Feedback Themes

1. Product Quality & Durability

- "Great quality, met my expectations."
- "Durable and feels premium."

👉 Customers find the product strong, reliable, and well-made.

2. Ease of Use & Performance

- "User-friendly and easy to set up."
- "Performance is fast and reliable."

👉 The product is simple to use, with good performance.

3. Value & Design

- "Value for money, worth it."
- "Design is sleek and modern."

👉 Customers appreciate affordability combined with stylish design.

4. Service & Packaging

- "Customer support was very helpful."
- "Packaging was eco-friendly and neat."

👉 Good customer care and eco-conscious packaging enhance brand image.

5. Recommendation Potential

- "Would definitely recommend to others."

👉 Strong word-of-mouth potential and high satisfaction overall.

⚡ Improvement Areas

Battery Life

- "Could improve battery life."

👉 The only notable area of concern. Extending battery longevity or offering clearer usage tips could significantly boost satisfaction.

✅ **Overall Summary:** Customers are very satisfied with the product's quality, ease of use, design, value, and customer support, and many are willing to recommend it. The main improvement opportunity lies in enhancing battery life to match the otherwise premium experience.

****

That's an action plan, ready in minutes.

C. Social Media Content Calendar

Generating months of posts doesn't need to be a headache.

Example Prompt

"Create a 7-day Instagram content calendar for a fitness brand that targets working moms. Include captions, hashtags, and post types."

Note: I've used the prompt for 7 days for brevity. You can create a content calendar for a month, quarter or a whole year.

AI Output Would be

****

Got it ✅ Let's make a 7-day Instagram content calendar for your fitness brand targeting working moms.
This plan balances motivation, practical tips, relatability, and subtle brand promotion.

📅 7-Day Instagram Content Calendar – Fitness for Working Moms

Day 1 – Monday Motivation (Image/Quote Post)

Caption:

"Strong moms, strong weeks 💪✨ You don't need hours — you just need to start.
What's one goal you're setting for yourself this week?"

Hashtags: #FitMomLife #WorkingMoms #MondayMotivation #StrongMomsStrongKids

Day 2 – Quick Workout (Reel)

Caption:

"Too busy for the gym? Try this 10-minute no-equipment workout you can do before the kids wake up 🕒.
Save this for tomorrow morning! 🙌"

Hashtags: #10MinuteWorkout #BusyMomFitness #FitMomHacks #HomeWorkoutMoms

Day 3 – Healthy Eating (Carousel)

Caption:

"3 easy snack swaps every busy mom will love 🥑🍎
👉 Slide through for quick, energy-boosting options.
Which one are you trying first?"

Hashtags: #HealthyMomSnacks #BusyMomHacks #MomLifeBalance #FuelYourBody

Day 4 – Relatable Moment (Story + Poll)

Caption:

"Morning workout or evening workout? 🌞🌙
Vote now!"
Hashtags: #MomFitnessJourney #FitMomCommunity #WorkingMomLife

Day 5 – Transformation/Success Story (Image or Reel)
Caption:
"Meet Sarah 👩 — a full-time accountant + mom of 2.
She started with just 15 minutes/day and now feels stronger, more energized, and more confident than ever ❤️.
If she can do it, so can you ✨."
Hashtags: #RealMomStories #FitMomInspiration #MomTransformation #StrongNotBusy

Day 6 – Family Fitness (Reel)
Caption:
"Turn playtime into workout time! 👶🤸
Here's a fun kid-friendly workout you can do together.
Fitness + bonding = double win ❤️."
Hashtags: #WorkoutWithKids #FamilyFitnessFun #MomLifeStrong #ActiveMoms

Day 7 – Self-Care Sunday (Image/Carousel)
Caption:
"Reminder: Rest is part of the process 🌸
Take today to recharge your body and mind.
What's your favourite self-care ritual, mama?"
Hashtags: #SelfCareForMoms #SundayReset #FitLifeMoms #MindfulMom

✅ This 7-day plan ensures:

- Motivation (Day 1 & 7)
- Practical fitness (Day 2 & 6)
- Nutrition tips (Day 3)
- Engagement & relatability (Day 4)
- Community inspiration (Day 5)

****

Done! From motivation quotes to mini workout reels and diet tips - all planned.

Bonus: Tips to Make Prompting for Business Even More Powerful

- **Use context-rich prompts**. The more details you provide, the better the output would be.
- **Always review and edit**. Think of the AI as a co-writer, not a mind reader.
- **Experiment with formats** - bullet points, tables, markdowns.
- **Save your best prompts as templates** or create custom prompt libraries for reuse.

In Conclusion

Prompting for business is like having an invisible team of writers, analysts, and assistants. When done well, it boosts productivity, sharpens strategy, and elevates creativity.

So go ahead, prompt your way to smarter, faster, and more exciting business growth.

And remember, just like in school — the more questions you ask, the more you learn. So, remember the mantra is ask(A), prompt(P), tweak(T), repeat(R)! APTR...

End of Chapter Exercises

1. In the context of AI-assisted copywriting, which of the following strategies BEST ensures that product descriptions resonate with a target audience?

   a. Using generic adjectives to appeal to everyone

   b. Relying solely on AI's default suggestions without adjustments

   c. Incorporating audience-specific lifestyle and values into the prompt

   d. Minimizing the length of descriptions to under 50 words

2. Which aspect of branding is MOST improved by AI prompting according to the text?

   a. Manufacturing process efficiency

   b. Defining brand voice and messaging consistently

   c. Setting retail pricing

   d. Tracking competitor sales data

3. Why is it critical to avoid overly technical or patronizing language in prompts for brand voice guidelines aimed at senior citizens?

   a. Patronizing language reduces trust and engagement

   b. Seniors prefer complex tech explanations to feel challenged

   c. It improves SEO ranking on Google

   d. AI cannot generate responses for technical prompts

4. When generating SEO-focused content using AI, what is the PRIMARY advantage of long-tail keywords?

   a. They increase website aesthetic appeal

   b. They guarantee top ranking on Google instantly

   c. They allow for shorter meta descriptions

   d. They target highly specific search queries with lower competition

5. In market research prompting, why is creating detailed customer personas particularly valuable?
   a. It replaces the need for competitor analysis
   b. It allows AI to generate stock photos of target demographics
   c. It helps understand behaviors, motivations, and challenges for targeted solutions
   d. It ensures all customers are treated identically

6. According to the text, what differentiates competitive analysis via AI prompting from traditional methods?
   a. AI can fully replace strategic decision-making
   b. AI can provide structured SWOT comparisons quickly, highlighting gaps and opportunities
   c. AI automatically increases brand revenue
   d. AI ensures legal compliance in international markets

7. Which of the following BEST exemplifies automating repetitive tasks with AI prompting?
   a. Writing a unique product description from scratch every day
   b. Generating email follow-ups, meeting summaries, and social media calendars automatically
   c. Hiring additional staff to handle repetitive emails
   d. Reading SEO reports manually

8. In creating a social media content calendar with AI, why is balance between motivation, practicality, relatability, and brand promotion important?
   a. It maximizes engagement across multiple audience needs and touchpoints
   b. It ensures AI generates content faster

c. It guarantees viral posts

d. It eliminates the need for human review

9. Which statement about fine-tuning AI prompts for business tasks is MOST accurate based on the text?

   a. Fine-tuning is unnecessary because AI can read minds

   b. Detailed, context-rich prompts result in better, more relevant outputs

   c. Prompts should always be vague to encourage creativity

   d. Fine-tuning guarantees perfect output without human editing

10. What is the underlying principle emphasized for effective prompting in business?

    a. Ask questions, prompt AI, tweak output, repeat (APTR)

    b. Only focus on SEO and ignore branding

    c. Avoid templates and libraries; always start from scratch

    d. Trust AI output without review

12. Prompting for Education

Artificial Intelligence, especially when guided with good prompts, is like having a super-teacher in your pocket. The beauty is that it can adapt, explain, quiz, and even cheer you on while you learn. But to really use it well, you need to know how to "prompt" it properly. Today, we'll explore three magical areas where prompting makes education powerful:

1. Personalized tutoring
2. Curriculum and quiz generation
3. Language learning with AI

Let's go one by one, in detail.

1. Personalized Tutoring

Imagine this: You're struggling with fractions. Your school teacher explained it once, but your brain is still saying, "Wait... ⅔ of what now?" This is where AI tutoring comes in.

When you prompt an AI correctly, it can act like a private tutor, giving you step-by-step guidance at your own pace.

How does this work?

A student can type: "Explain fractions to me like I'm 8 years old. Use pizza slices as examples."

AI Output Would be

****

Alright, let's make fractions super fun using pizza 🍕 — because who doesn't love pizza?

🍕 **What is a fraction?**

A fraction is a way to show a part of a whole.

Think of a pizza cut into slices. The whole pizza is "1."
Each slice is a fraction of that pizza.

Example 1: Half (1/2)

If your pizza is cut into 2 equal slices and you eat 1 slice, you've eaten:

1 out of 2 slices = 1/2

We say "one-half."

Example 2: Quarters (1/4)

Now imagine your pizza is cut into 4 equal slices.

If you eat 1 slice, you've eaten:

1 out of 4 slices = 1/4

We say "one-quarter."

If you eat 2 slices, that's 2/4, which is the same as 1/2 (half a pizza!).

Example 3: Eighths (1/8)

Suppose your pizza is cut into 8 equal slices.

If you eat 3 slices, that's:

3 out of 8 = 3/8 of the pizza.

The more slices the pizza is cut into, the smaller each fraction becomes!

Easy Way to Remember

- The top number (numerator) tells how many slices you have.
- The bottom number (denominator) tells how many slices the whole pizza was cut into.

Example: 3/8 = 3 slices out of 8 total.

So next time you're eating pizza with friends, you'll secretly be a math wizard with fractions!

****

The magic lies in the prompt. By asking the AI to explain "like I'm 8 years old," the student tailors the complexity of the explanation.

Benefits of Personalized Tutoring with Prompts:

- **Customized learning speed:** If you say, "Don't move to the next step until I say I understand," the AI slows down for you.

- **Different learning styles:** A visual learner can prompt: "Explain photosynthesis with a diagram." A story lover can say: "Teach me about photosynthesis as if it's a fairy tale."

- **Encouragement and motivation:** You can even prompt: "Act like a cheerful coach and encourage me after each answer." Suddenly, learning feels less like a chore and more like a game.

Example Scenario

A 12-year-old struggling with history could ask:
"Can you explain the French Revolution like a comic strip story with heroes and villains?"

AI Output Would be

****

Love this idea 😃 Let's turn the French Revolution into a fun, comic-strip-style story with heroes, villains, and dramatic scenes.

📖 The French Revolution as a Comic Strip

🎭 Scene 1: The Kingdom of Cake

👑 King Louis XVI and 👑 Queen Marie Antoinette live in a palace (Versailles), eating cake, wearing wigs, and spending loads of money.
Meanwhile...
😟 Ordinary people (farmers, workers, poor families) struggle with high taxes and hunger.

Villains: The King & Queen's extravagance + unfair taxes.
Heroes in waiting: The common people ("The Third Estate").

🎭 Scene 2: The People Rise Up

💥 The poor (Third Estate) say: “We’ve had enough!”

They form a group called the National Assembly and promise to write a new constitution.

This is like the heroes gathering their team in a superhero movie.

🎭 Scene 3: The Storming of the Bastille (1789)

👫 The people storm the Bastille prison (a symbol of the king’s power).

⚔️ They break down the doors, free prisoners, and take weapons.

This becomes the spark of the revolution!

Hero moment: The crowd defeats a symbol of tyranny.

🎭 Scene 4: The Villains Lose Power

The National Assembly makes new rules:

- Nobles lose special privileges.
- Feudalism is abolished.
- The Declaration of the Rights of Man says everyone has rights.

🏰 The King and Queen try to escape but are caught.

Crowd: “No more kings eating cake while we starve!”

🎭 Scene 5: The Guillotine Falls

⚖️ King Louis XVI is put on trial.

❌ Verdict: guilty of betraying the people.

🔪 He is executed with the guillotine in 1793.

Later, Marie Antoinette meets the same fate.

The heroes cheer-but the story isn’t over...

🎭 Scene 6: Enter a New Villain – Robespierre

Robespierre (a revolutionary leader) first seems like a hero, fighting for justice.

But then...

😈 He becomes too strict and starts the Reign of Terror.

Thousands are executed — even innocent people.

Villain twist: A hero turned tyrant.

🎭 **Scene 7: A New Hero Rises – Napoleon**

Out of the chaos, a young general named Napoleon Bonaparte takes charge.
⚔️ He promises order, stability, and victories.
He crowns himself Emperor, ending the Revolution but shaping France's future.

Hero or Villain? That's up for debate!

💥 Comic-Style Cast List

- Heroes: The People, National Assembly, early revolutionaries.
- Villains: King Louis XVI, Marie Antoinette, and later Robespierre.
- Anti-Hero: Napoleon (both saviour and ruler).

👉 And that's the French Revolution — a dramatic comic-book story of heroes, villains, betrayal, and transformation.
****

See? Prompting turns a boring textbook chapter into a lively adventure.

2. Curriculum and Quiz Generation

Teachers, parents, and even self-learners often need structured learning paths. This is where prompting can shine as a curriculum designer.

Curriculum Creation with Prompts

Let's say a parent wants to teach their 10-year-old child about Space Science for a month.

Example Prompt

"Create a 4-week curriculum on Space Science for a 10-year-old. Include weekly topics, daily activities, and one fun project per week."

The AI can then design something like

****

Here's a 4-week Space Science curriculum designed for a curious 10-year-old! It balances learning, fun, and hands-on projects, with simple daily activities.

🪐 4-Week Space Science Curriculum for Kids (Age 10)

Week 1: Introduction to Space & The Solar System

Goal: Learn what space is, planets, and our solar system.

- Day 1: What is space? Watch a short kids' video on outer space.
- Day 2: Learn about the Sun and its importance. Draw a big bright sun.
- Day 3: Explore the 8 planets – make a list of them in order.
- Day 4: Compare planets (size, distance, temperature).
- Day 5: Learn about moons (focus on Earth's moon).
- Day 6: Make a solar system mobile (paper planets hanging on strings).
- Day 7 (Project): Build a Solar System Model (using clay, paper, or even fruit/balls to represent planets).

Week 2: Earth, Moon & Space Travel

Goal: Understand Earth in space, the Moon, and how humans travel beyond Earth.

- Day 1: Learn why Earth is special (air, water, life).
- Day 2: Explore the Moon's phases – draw them in a notebook.
- Day 3: Watch a video of the Moon landing (Neil Armstrong).
- Day 4: Learn about astronauts (suits, training, space food).
- Day 5: Make a simple moon crater experiment (drop small rocks into flour topped with cocoa powder).
- Day 6: Roleplay "A Day as an Astronaut" (pretend eating space food, floating in space).
- Day 7 (Project): Moon Journal – Track the Moon's phase for a week and create a small diary.

Week 3: Stars, Galaxies & Beyond

Goal: Learn about stars, constellations, and galaxies.

- Day 1: What are stars? Learn why they twinkle.

- Day 2: Explore constellations – pick 3 to memorize (Orion, Big Dipper, Cassiopeia).
- Day 3: Learn about the Milky Way galaxy.
- Day 4: Make a "constellation viewer" with a toilet paper roll and pinholes.
- Day 5: Explore other galaxies and the concept of black holes (kid-friendly videos).
- Day 6: Glow-in-the-dark star art (make a night sky with constellations).
- Day 7 (Project): DIY Star Map – Draw your favourite constellations on black paper with white chalk/paint.

Week 4: Space Exploration & The Future

Goal: Learn about rockets, satellites, and the future of space.

- Day 1: What are satellites? Learn how they help us (GPS, weather).
- Day 2: Rockets – how they work (simple explanation: push + fuel).
- Day 3: International Space Station – see pictures, learn what happens there.
- Day 4: Mars exploration – rovers like Curiosity & Perseverance.
- Day 5: Future missions – Artemis, SpaceX, living on Mars.
- Day 6: Build a simple paper rocket and launch with a straw.
- Day 7 (Project): Design Your Own Space Mission – Draw a rocket, planet destination, and explain what you'd discover.

✨ **End Goal:** By the end of 4 weeks, the child will know about planets, moons, stars, astronauts, rockets, and the future of space — with hands-on projects to keep it exciting!

****

Notice how prompts let you generate age-specific, goal-oriented, and fun learning plans in minutes.

Quiz Generation with Prompts

Now comes the testing part – quizzes! Teachers spend hours designing quizzes, but prompts make it effortless.

Example Prompt

A teacher could type: "Create a fill-in-the-blank quiz for Grade 5 on water cycles."

AI Output Would Be

****

Here's a Grade 5 Fill-in-the-Blank Quiz on the Water Cycle:

🌊 **Water Cycle Quiz (Grade 5)**

Name: ____________________ Date: ____________

1. The water cycle is also called the ________________ cycle.
2. When water from oceans, lakes, or rivers changes into water vapor, the process is called ________________.
3. Plants release water vapor into the air through their leaves in a process called ________________.
4. When water vapor cools down and turns back into liquid droplets, it is called ________________.
5. These droplets gather together to form ________________ in the sky.
6. When clouds become heavy, water falls back to Earth as ________________.
7. Rain, snow, sleet, and hail are all forms of ________________.
8. Water that soaks into the ground is called ________________ water.
9. Water that flows over the surface of the land and returns to rivers, lakes, and oceans is called ________________.
10. The water cycle is important because it moves and cleans ________________ all over the Earth.

✅ Answer Key (for teacher/parent use):

1. Hydrologic
2. Evaporation
3. Transpiration
4. Condensation
5. Clouds

6. Precipitation
7. Precipitation
8. Groundwater
9. Runoff
10. Water

****

Want to make studying fun? Here you go...

Example Prompt

"Turn a math quiz on percentages into a treasure hunt story. Each correct answer gives me a clue to the treasure."

And voila! Math turns into an adventure game.

AI Output Would be

****

Alright, let's turn your math quiz on percentages into a fun treasure hunt story 🏴‍☠️✨.

📜 The Treasure of Golden Island

You are an explorer searching for the hidden treasure of Golden Island. To unlock each clue, you must solve a percentage riddle. Get it right, and the map reveals your next step.

🔎 Clue 1 – The Secret Map

You find an old chest with a map. The lock says:
"A shop gives a 25% discount on a bicycle that costs $200. What is the new price?"

👉 Solve it to open the chest!
(Answer: $150. The chest opens, revealing the map with the next clue.)

🔎 Clue 2 – The River of Numbers

The map shows a wide river. To build a bridge, solve:

"There are 40 apples, and 10% are rotten. How many are rotten?"

👉 Solve to cross the river.
(Answer: 4 apples. You cross safely to the other side.)

🔎 **Clue 3 – The Mountain Gate**
At the base of a tall mountain, a stone door asks:
"In a class of 60 students, 50% are girls. How many are girls?"

👉 Solve to open the mountain gate.
(Answer: 30 girls. The gate opens to a glowing tunnel.)

🔎 **Clue 4 – The Hidden Village**
Inside the tunnel, villagers offer help if you solve:
"You scored 80 out of 100 in a test. What percentage is that?"

👉 Solve to gain their help.
(Answer: 80%. The villagers hand you a golden key.)

🔎 **Clue 5 – The Final Treasure**
You reach the treasure cave. The lock says:
"A jacket costs $120. It is increased by 10%. What is the new price?"

👉 Solve to unlock the treasure.
(Answer: $132. The lock clicks open.)

🎉 **You Found the Treasure!**
Gold coins, jewels, and a shiny crown are yours! 🏆💎
You solved the percentage riddles and became the hero of Golden Island.
****

3. Language Learning with AI

Learning a new language can feel intimidating. But prompts allow AI to become your language buddy, patient teacher, and roleplay partner all in one.

How Prompts Help in Language Learning

a. Vocabulary Practice

Example Prompt

"Give me 10 new French words today, each with an example sentence and a fun emoji."

AI Output Would be

****

Parfait! 🌟 Here are 10 new French words with example sentences and fun emojis for today's practice:

1. Le chat (the cat) 🐱

👉 Le chat dort sur le canapé. (The cat is sleeping on the couch.)

2. La pomme (the apple) 🍎

👉 Je mange une pomme rouge. (I am eating a red apple.)

3. L'école (the school) 🏫

👉 Les enfants vont à l'école le matin. (The children go to school in the morning.)

4. La maison (the house) 🏠

👉 Notre maison est très confortable. (Our house is very comfortable.)

5. Le soleil (the sun) ☀️

👉 Le soleil brille dans le ciel bleu. (The sun is shining in the blue sky.)

6. La voiture (the car) 🚗

👉 Mon père conduit une voiture bleue. (My dad drives a blue car.)

7. Le livre (the book) 📖

👉 Je lis un livre intéressant. (I am reading an interesting book.)

8. L'oiseau (the bird) 🐦

👉 L'oiseau chante dans l'arbre. (The bird is singing in the tree.)

9. La mer (the sea) 🌊

👉 Nous nageons dans la mer. (We are swimming in the sea.)

10. Le gâteau (the cake) 🎂

👉 Elle prépare un gâteau au chocolat. (She is making a chocolate cake.)

****

b. Roleplaying

Example Prompt

"Pretend you are a waiter in a Paris café. I will order food in French. Correct me if I make mistakes: Je voudrais dus frites et de poisson avec un coca, s'il vous plaît."

AI Output Would be

****

👨‍🍳🍽️ Ah, parfait, monsieur/madame! Juste une petite correction :

You wrote:
"Je voudrais dus frites et de poisson avec un coca, s'il vous plaît."

✅ Correct version:
"Je voudrais des frites et du poisson avec un coca, s'il vous plaît."

- dus ❌ → should be des (plural article for frites 🍟)
- de poisson ❌ → should be du poisson (partitive article for fish 🐟)

So the waiter would smile and say:
👉 Très bien, je vous apporte des frites, du poisson et un coca !

Voulez-vous essayer de commander encore une fois, mais cette fois sans erreur ? 😃

****

c. Grammar Drills

Example Prompt

"Explain past tense in Spanish with 3 examples. Then give me 5 sentences to practice."

AI Output Would be

****

Great question! Let's dive into Spanish past tense ✨

In Spanish, there are two main simple past tenses that learners start with:

1. El Pretérito (Preterite)
- Used for completed actions in the past.
- Example: Ayer comí pizza. → "Yesterday I ate pizza."

2. El Imperfecto (Imperfect)
- Used for ongoing, repeated, or background actions in the past.
- Example: Cuando era niño, jugaba al fútbol. → "When I was a child, I used to play soccer."

3. Combining both (Preterite + Imperfect)
- Often, the imperfect sets the scene and the preterite tells what happened.
- Example: Yo estudiaba cuando mi amigo llamó. → "I was studying when my friend called."

✍ Now, your practice: Translate these 5 sentences into Spanish (using past tense).

1. I went to the market yesterday.
2. When I was young, I used to read a lot of books.
3. We were eating dinner when the phone rang.
4. She lived in Madrid for two years.
5. It was raining, and we walked with umbrellas.

****

d. Cultural Immersion

Example Prompt

"Teach me common Japanese phrases used during a festival. Add fun facts about their traditions."

AI Output Would be

****

Perfect! Let's step into the lively world of Japanese matsuri (festivals) 🎆🎐. Festivals in Japan are full of color, music, food stalls, and traditional rituals.

I'll teach you some common Japanese phrases you'll hear or use at a matsuri, and sprinkle in fun cultural facts.

🎏 **Common Japanese Festival Phrases**

1. いらっしゃいませ！ (Irasshaimase!) - "Welcome!"

👉 Said by shopkeepers or food stall vendors.

🌸 Fun fact: Every vendor enthusiastically yells this to grab attention, often in a rhythmic chant-like way.

2. これください (Kore kudasai) - "This one, please."

👉 Use this when buying food or toys from stalls.

🌸 Fun fact: At festivals, you'll find stalls selling takoyaki (octopus balls), yakisoba, and candied apples.

3. いくらですか？ (Ikura desu ka?) - "How much is it?"

👉 Always handy when shopping!

🌸 Fun fact: Many festival games, like goldfish scooping (kingyo sukui), cost only a few hundred yen.

4. たのしい！ (Tanoshii!) - "So much fun!"

👉 Express your excitement during parades, dances, or fireworks.

🌸 Fun fact: The Awa Odori Festival in Tokushima features dancers chanting and moving in sync — tourists often join in!

5. おみくじをひきたいです (Omikuji o hikitai desu) - "I want to draw a fortune slip."

👉 Said at shrine festivals when drawing a fortune.

🌸 Fun fact: If your fortune (omikuji) is bad, you tie it to a tree at the shrine so the bad luck won't follow you.

6. すごい！ (Sugoi!) - "Amazing!"

👉 Shout this when you see fireworks (hanabi) explode in the night sky.

🌸 Fun fact: Summer fireworks festivals (hanabi taikai) are so popular that people reserve spots hours in advance with picnic mats.

🎏 **Bonus Fun Facts About Japanese Festivals:**

- Many people wear yukata (summer kimono) during summer matsuri.
- Stalls often sell masks of anime characters and traditional figures like foxes (kitsune).
- The Gion Matsuri in Kyoto is over 1,100 years old and one of the most famous festivals in Japan.
- Some festivals involve carrying huge shrines (mikoshi) through the streets while chanting.

✨ **Quick Practice for You:**

Try saying in Japanese what you'd do at a matsuri! For example:

- "I want takoyaki, please." → たこやきをください (Takoyaki o kudasai).

****

More Examples

If you prompt: "Help me practice Spanish greetings like a friend" the AI might chat casually:

AI Output Would be

****

¡Perfecto! Let's practice Spanish greetings like two friends chatting. I'll act like your Spanish-speaking buddy, and you can reply however you like. If you make a mistake, I'll gently correct you. Ready? 😄

👋 Me: ¡Hola! ¿Cómo estás, amigo/a?

👉 Your turn: reply in Spanish.

****

This way you can chat casually with AI in Spanish.

Want humour?

Prompt: "Teach me German colors like a comedian."

AI Output Would be

****

😄 Alright, let's make learning German colors fun — like a comedian on stage teaching you! Get ready to laugh and learn! 🎭

🎤 "Ladies and gentlemen, willkommen to the German Color Comedy Show! Today we'll paint your brain with colors so bright, you'll need sunglasses. 😎"

🌈 **Colors in German (with a funny twist):**

1. **Rot** (red) ❤️
"Rot is like your face when you realize you just called your teacher mom by accident."
2. **Blau** (blue) 💙
"Blau is the sky... unless you live in Germany, where it's gray half the year. 🌧️"
3. **Grün** (green) 💚
"Grün is grass... except when your neighbour's dog visits. 🐶💩"
4. **Gelb** (yellow) 💛
"Gelb is like sunshine... or the banana you forgot in your backpack for three weeks. 🍌"
5. **Schwarz** (black) 🖤
"Schwarz is the color of your soul when Wi-Fi stops working. 📵"
6. **Weiß** (white) 🤍
"Weiß is snow... or your face when you see the electricity bill. ❄️😱"
7. **Orange** (orange) 🧡
"Orange is... well, orange. Even Germans gave up on inventing a new word. 🍊"
8. **Rosa** (pink) 💖
"Rosa is love, cuteness, and unicorns... unless you're a tough guy, then it's just camouflage in Barbie's house. 🦄"
9. **Lila** (purple) 💜
"Lila is mysterious... like your grandma's couch nobody's allowed to sit on."
10. **Braun** (brown) 🤎
"Braun is chocolate... or mud. You decide which one you step in. 🍫👟"

🎤 "And that's the end of our colourful German comedy show! Now, who's ready to shout some colors like a rockstar?" 🎸
****

Why this works

Prompts make language learning less robotic. Instead of memorizing dry lists, you learn through interaction, context, and play.

Wrapping It All Up

So, prompting in education isn't about just asking random questions. It's about guiding AI like a smart assistant teacher to:

1. Adjust lessons to your style (personalized tutoring)
2. Create structured paths and assessments (curriculum and quiz generation)
3. Make learning interactive, cultural, and fun (language learning with AI)

Think of it this way: The better you prompt, the better your AI becomes at teaching you. It's like training your own genie — but instead of three wishes, you get unlimited answers, explanations, and quizzes.

And hey, the best part? This genie doesn't get tired when you ask the same question 10 times.

End of Chapter Exercises

1. A student asks AI: *"Explain fractions like I'm 8 years old using pizza slices."* Why is this prompt considered highly effective for **personalized tutoring**?

   a. It requires AI to generate diagrams only

   b. It avoids using any contextual examples

   c. It uses metaphor and real-life examples familiar to the learner

   d. It ensures AI outputs in advanced mathematical notation

2. Which of the following BEST demonstrates prompting for **different learning styles**?

   a. "Summarize Newton's laws in under 10 words."

   b. "Explain photosynthesis with a diagram for a visual learner."

   c. "List random facts about gravity."

   d. "Give me the definition of inertia from a physics textbook."

3. A teacher prompts AI: *"Create a 4-week Space Science curriculum for a 10-year-old with daily activities and weekly projects."* Which feature of effective educational prompting does this BEST illustrate?

   a. Chunking content into structured, age-appropriate sequences

   b. Using prompts that force AI to produce only multiple-choice quizzes

   c. Demanding AI responses in academic journal format

   d. Ensuring the curriculum avoids hands-on activities

4. Why is prompting AI to "act like a cheerful coach and encourage me after each answer" pedagogically valuable?

   a. It minimizes knowledge retention

   b. It avoids interactive feedback

   c. It ensures AI outputs only long theoretical essays

   d. It introduces affective (emotional) support to learning

5. During quiz generation, a teacher asks: *"Turn a math quiz on percentages into a treasure hunt story where each correct answer unlocks a clue."* This demonstrates which principle of AI educational prompting?

   a. Removal of contextual clues to increase difficulty

   b. Exclusive reliance on fill-in-the-blank tests

   c. Narrative gamification of assessments

   d. Avoidance of interactivity in assessments

6. A learner prompts: *"Pretend you are a waiter in a Paris café. I'll order food in French, and correct me if I make mistakes."* Why is this more effective than asking "Give me 10 French food words"?

   a. It reduces learning complexity by skipping grammar

   b. It ensures vocabulary is memorized without context

   c. It avoids interactive practice, focusing on rote learning

   d. It embeds corrective feedback in an authentic, roleplay scenario

7. Which of the following prompts BEST combines **grammar drills** with **active practice** in language learning?

   a. "Translate these 5 sentences into Spanish using the past tense."

   b. "List the rules of past tense in Spanish without examples."

   c. "Give me random Spanish words."

   d. "Provide a Spanish dictionary entry for the word 'comer.'"

8. Why does prompting AI to include *fun cultural facts* alongside festival vocabulary (e.g., Japanese matsuri phrases) enhance language learning?

   a. It distracts learners from grammar rules

   b. It avoids the need for memorization

   c. It deepens contextual and cultural immersion

   d. It reduces the variety of vocabulary exposure

9. If a student asks AI: *"Teach me German colors like a comedian,"* which underlying instructional principle is at play?
   a. Multimodal sensory input
   b. Elimination of context in language teaching
   c. Strict adherence to textbook definitions
   d. Humour as a motivational engagement tool

10. The text concludes that prompting in education is MOST powerful because:
    a. AI can replace all teachers entirely
    b. Effective prompts adapt teaching to style, structure, and interactivity
    c. Prompts always generate perfect answers without error
    d. AI requires no fine-tuning for different learners

13. Prompting for Creative Writing & Content

Creative writing with AI is like having a magical pen that never runs out of ink. But this pen listens to your prompts, your imagination, and your direction. To make the most of it, you need to learn how to ask — and what to ask. Let's break it into three wonderful subtopics.

1. Fiction and Poetry Generation

Creative writing thrives on imagination. With AI prompting, you can turn a plain idea into an entire story or poem. The trick is in the specificity of your prompt.

Think of it like this: if you tell your AI, "Write me a story," it's like telling a chef, "Cook me food." You'll get something, but not what you were craving. Instead, you must say:

"Write a story about a lonely astronaut on Mars who finds a hidden library filled with books from Earth."

Now the AI has a starting point, a theme, and a mood!

For fiction, you can control:

- **Genre:** fantasy, sci-fi, romance, mystery.
- **Tone:** dark, humorous, whimsical, serious.
- **Point of view:** first-person, third-person, omniscient narrator.

Example Prompt

"Write a whimsical fairy tale about a dragon who wants to become a vegetarian chef, narrated in the style of a children's bedtime story."

This prompt tells the AI what to do, how to do it, and what mood to set.

AI Output Would be

****

🐉 The Dragon Who Cooked Carrots

Once upon a giggle and a yawn, high in the misty mountains, lived a dragon named Grumblebelly. Why was he called that? Well, because his tummy made loud Grrrrrrr! noises whenever he smelled roasted knights or sizzling sheep.

But here's the twist — Grumblebelly didn't like roasted knights or sizzling sheep. He didn't even like crispy goats! He wanted to be... 🥕 a vegetarian chef!

Yes, you heard right. A dragon who breathed fire, but dreamed of steaming broccoli instead of barbecuing villagers.

One sunny morning, Grumblebelly waddled into the village market. The people screamed, "Aaaaah! Dragon!" and dropped their baskets of carrots and cabbages.
Grumblebelly sighed, "No, no, no! I don't want to eat you. I want your vegetables!"

But the villagers didn't believe him. So, he came up with a plan.

He set up the first ever Dragon Café right in the forest. The sign read:
✨ Grumblebelly's Garden Kitchen — No Humans on the Menu! ✨

The first dish he made was Carrot Soufflé à la Dragon. He used his fiery breath to bake it perfectly golden.
Next, he roasted pumpkins so sweet they made squirrels do the cha-cha. 🐿️💃
And for dessert, he invented Banana Flambé, with a little poof! of fire. 🍌🔥

One brave little girl tiptoed into the café and tried his soup.
"Hmm... This is delicious!" she said.

Word spread quickly. Soon, even the king waddled in, crown wobbling on his head.

And do you know what happened?
The villagers stopped running. They started eating! The whole kingdom gathered every evening in the Dragon Café. Knights put down their swords to pick up spoons. Farmers brought fresh veggies as gifts.

Grumblebelly's tummy stopped grumbling.
And at last… he was full of happiness, not meat. 💚

And so, children, if you ever hear a dragon's belly go Grrrrrrr, don't be scared. He might just be craving a salad. 🥗🐉

✨ **The End. Goodnight, sleep tight.** 🌙
****

For poetry, prompts can focus on:

- **Style:** haiku (a very short form of poetry that originated in Japan), free verse (a type of poetry that doesn't follow traditional rules of rhyme, meter, or line length), sonnet (a type of poem that has a very specific structure and is usually 14 lines long).
- **Theme:** love, loss, seasons, self-discovery.
- **Imagery:** ask for metaphors, vivid sensory descriptions.

Example Prompt

"Write a haiku about the feeling of holding hands with someone you love for the first time."

AI Output Would be

****

Fingers intertwine,
nervous sparks bloom into warmth,
the world disappears.

****

The main point: the clearer and more playful your prompt, the better the story or poem you'll receive.

2. World-Building and Dialogue

Now let's go deeper. A story is not just a plot. It's the world and the characters who live inside it. Prompts can be designed to flesh out entire universes.

a. World-Building

Imagine you want to create a fantasy world like Tolkien or a dystopian city like George Orwell. Instead of asking vaguely, be specific.

Example Prompt

"Describe a futuristic city in the year 3025 where humans and robots live together, but only robots are allowed to vote. Explain the architecture, the culture, and how humans feel about this system."

AI Output Would be

****

In the year 3025, the city of Neonhaven rises like a glowing jewel against the sky. Its architecture is a fusion of glass, bio-metal, and living plants — skyscrapers twist upward like giant vines, their walls made of transparent solar panels that shift color with the sun. Floating bridges connect towers, and maglev pods zip silently along air-rails, carrying citizens — both human and robotic — through the vertical city. Robots maintain the structures, ensuring nothing ever decays, while humans contribute creativity, art, and emotional labour.

Culturally, Neonhaven thrives on a strange duality. Robots hold the political power: only they can vote, on the grounds that their decisions are free from greed, bias, or impulsive emotions. They pass laws, design city policies, and decide how resources are distributed. Festivals are still communal, though — robots and humans gather in luminous plazas where holographic art dances in the air and music blends mechanical rhythms with human voices.

Humans run restaurants, design fashion, and tell stories, while robots handle governance, infrastructure, and justice.

For many humans, this system stings. Some feel relieved — trusting the robots to avoid corruption and war — but others feel silenced, frustrated that their voices matter only in culture, not in politics. In secret cafés hidden in the shadowy under-levels of the city, whispers of resistance stir. A new generation of humans is asking: If robots were built to serve humanity, why does humanity now serve the system of robots?

And so, Neonhaven glows: dazzling, harmonious on the surface, but carrying quiet human unrest just beneath its radiant skin. 🌃🤖✨
****

See what's happening here? The AI is not just spitting out random buildings. It's exploring politics, feelings, and culture — because the prompt asked for it.

b. Dialogue

Dialogue makes characters feel alive. Instead of asking for "a conversation," give context. Who is speaking? What's their mood? What's the conflict?

Example Prompt

"Write a dialogue between a queen who wants peace and her hot-headed general who insists on war. Set it in the war chamber as thunder roars outside."

Now the AI will produce tension-filled lines that sound natural and dramatic.

AI Output Would be

****

Here's your scene:

[Setting: The war chamber. A storm rages outside, lightning flashing through tall windows. The Queen sits at the head of a long wooden table, her crown glinting faintly in the candlelight. Maps of kingdoms are spread before her. The General, armoured and restless, paces like a caged wolf.]

General: (slamming his fist on the table) My Queen, every moment we hesitate, our enemies sharpen their blades! Give me the order, and I will march tonight.

Queen: (calm, though thunder shakes the chamber) And tomorrow, what then? A hundred widows in the streets? A thousand children without fathers? Tell me, General, who will fight their sorrow?

General: (voice rising) Better sorrow than chains! Mercy is weakness. Peace is a lullaby before slaughter.

Queen: (rising slowly, her gaze piercing) Peace is not weakness. It is mastery. To hold the sword and choose not to strike — that is strength.

General: (snorts, pacing faster) Words! While you weave poems, their armies grow. They mock us. They see your mercy as cowardice.

Queen: (steps closer, speaking softly but firmly) Let them mock. A throne does not tremble because the jester laughs.

General: (growling) Then what would you have me do? Sit idle? Watch them fortify, until they descend upon us like wolves?

Queen: (placing a hand on his armoured shoulder) I would have you prepare, but not provoke. Guard our borders, shield our people — but do not burn the world because you cannot master your fury.

General: (hesitates, torn, his jaw clenched) And if they strike first?

Queen: (looking out the window as lightning illuminates her face) Then, my General, we will answer as storm answers silence — with thunder so fierce the earth remembers. But until that day... we hold.

[The chamber falls silent except for the rumble of distant thunder. The General lowers his head, unwilling but swayed. The Queen returns to her seat, her hand steady on the map.]

****

Teachers' tip: If dialogue sounds too flat, you can refine the prompt. Say, "Make the dialogue witty," or "Use Shakespearean English," or even "Keep sentences short and snappy like in a modern TV drama."

3. Blog Outlines, YouTube Scripts, and Social Media Posts

Here's where prompting meets the real world. Creative content is not just for novels — it's also for online platforms where attention spans are short and competition is high.

1. Blog Outlines

Instead of staring at a blank screen, prompt the AI to draft an outline.

Example Prompt

"Create a detailed outline for a blog post titled '5 Ways to Stay Motivated While Working from Home.' Include an introduction, subheadings, and a conclusion."

AI Output Would be

****

Here's a detailed outline for your blog post:

Outline: 5 Ways to Stay Motivated While Working from Home
Introduction

- Hook: Start with a relatable scenario — pyjamas, coffee in hand, laptop on the couch, and yet... zero motivation.
- Acknowledge the perks and challenges of working from home.
- State purpose: This post will share five practical, science-backed, and easy-to-apply strategies to stay motivated while working remotely.

1. Create a Dedicated Workspace

- Why it matters: Helps your brain separate "work mode" from "relax mode."
- Examples: A desk by a window, a small corner with good lighting, or even just a consistent spot at the dining table.
- Tips: Keep it tidy, add plants, personalize it with things that inspire you.

2. Stick to a Morning Routine

- Why it matters: A morning ritual signals your body and mind that it's time to get productive.
- Examples: Exercise, shower, make coffee, write down daily goals.
- Fun fact: Many successful entrepreneurs swear by morning routines.
- Quick tip: Lay out your clothes the night before, even if you're not leaving home.

3. Break Work into Manageable Chunks

- Why it matters: Large tasks feel overwhelming and can kill motivation.
- Strategy: Use the Pomodoro technique (25 min work + 5 min break).
- Examples: Break "write report" into "draft outline," "research stats," "write intro."
- Benefit: Each small win creates momentum.

4. Stay Connected with Others

- Why it matters: Working from home can get lonely, reducing motivation.
- Suggestions: Schedule virtual coffee chats, join coworking video calls, or check in with teammates daily.
- Pro tip: Use accountability buddies to keep each other on track.

5. Reward Yourself for Progress

- Why it matters: Positive reinforcement boosts motivation.
- Ideas: Enjoy a snack after finishing a task, take a short walk, or watch an episode of your favourite show after a productive session.
- Note: Rewards should match effort (big task = bigger reward).

Conclusion

- Recap the five tips.
- Reassure readers: Motivation dips are normal, but these strategies can help.
- End with encouragement: "Working from home isn't just about discipline — it's about designing a system that keeps you inspired."
- Call-to-action: Invite readers to share their own motivation hacks in the comments.

****

The AI gave you a skeleton structure. Now you can expand each section with more prompts like:

"Write a motivational introduction in a friendly, conversational tone."

"Give three scientific reasons why taking breaks improves productivity."

2. YouTube Scripts

YouTube thrives on personality. Prompts should tell the AI the role and vibe.

Example Prompt

"Write a YouTube script for a 1-minute video where a cheerful tech reviewer explains the 1 smart home gadget of 2025. Add humour, simple analogies, and a call-to-action at the end."

AI Output Would be

****

Here's a lively 1-minute YouTube script for you 🎥:

[Intro: cheerful, upbeat music]

👋 "Hey everyone! Welcome back to Tech in a Minute! I'm [Your Name], your friendly neighbourhood gadget nerd who still thinks the toaster is judging me."

[Cut to gadget on table]

"Today, we're talking about the number one smart home gadget of 2025 — the Smart Fridge Butler 2.0! 🎉

This thing doesn't just keep your food cold... oh no, it's basically your kitchen's personal life coach.
Ran out of milk? It orders it for you. 🥛
Can't decide what to eat? It scans your fridge and suggests recipes — like a foodie psychic. 🔮
And get this — it shames you (politely) if you reach for ice cream at 2 a.m. 'Are you sure, buddy? Remember the treadmill you bought last year?' Thanks, fridge, I feel so seen."

[Quick demo clip: showing features]

"It even syncs with your smart oven and tells it when to preheat. Basically, it's like your grandma moved in — if your grandma had WiFi and a British accent." GB😄

[Outro: music builds]

"So, would you let a fridge boss you around? Drop your thoughts in the comments, smash that like button if you've ever been caught fridge-raiding at midnight, and don't forget to subscribe for more tech fun. Until next time — stay smart, stay curious!"

[End screen with cheerful wave]

****

The AI can even mimic the flow: intro → hook → explanation → CTA.

3. Social Media Posts

These need to be short, catchy, and scroll-stopping. Prompts must include tone, emotion, and sometimes even emojis.

Example Prompt

"Write a witty Instagram caption for a picture of a sunset over the ocean. Make it sound reflective but also playful. Add 3 popular hashtags."

AI Output Would be

****

"Proof that the ocean really knows how to show off at golden hour 🌅✨ … meanwhile I'm just here pretending it's all for me. 😉"

#SunsetVibes #OceanLove #GoldenHourGlow

****

Or:

"Create 2 tweet-sized posts about why reading fantasy novels is like traveling without a passport. Keep them witty and under 280 characters."

AI Output Would be

****

Here are two tweet-sized posts for you:

1.

Reading fantasy novels is like traveling without a passport: no security lines, no jet lag — just dragons, castles, and a seat upgrade straight into another world. 🐉📚✈️

2.

Who needs a passport when a fantasy book can take you across realms? One page = a boarding pass, one chapter = jet lag, one trilogy = permanent residency in another universe. 🌍✨

****

Notice how each prompt specifies platform, mood, and goal.

Wrapping It Up

Prompting for creative writing is like being both the director and the scriptwriter. The AI is your actor — talented, versatile, and ready to perform. But the quality of the performance depends on the directions you give.

- For fiction and poetry, focus on detail and mood.
- For world-building and dialogue, build context and conflict.
- For blogs, videos, and posts, specify audience, platform, and style.

And remember — don't be afraid to play! Sometimes the best stories come from the silliest prompts.

Teacher's Homework for You

Try giving AI this prompt:

"Write a poem from the perspective of a coffee mug who feels unappreciated in the kitchen."

I bet it will surprise you.

End of Chapter Exercises

1. A writer prompts: *"Write me a story."* Why does this often produce unsatisfying output compared to *"Write a whimsical fairy tale about a dragon who wants to be a vegetarian chef, narrated in the style of a children's bedtime story"*?

   a. The first lacks specificity in subject, tone, and style

   b. The first forces AI to generate overly technical language

   c. The second is ineffective because it restricts creativity

   d. The second removes narrative flow

2. Which of the following prompts BEST demonstrates **effective world-building**?

   a. "Describe a city."

   b. "Describe a futuristic city in the year 3025 where humans and robots live together, but only robots can vote. Include architecture, culture, and human emotions."

   c. "Write about architecture in a random world."

   d. "Explain the meaning of the word 'city' in 100 words."

3. Why does the example prompt *"Write a dialogue between a queen who wants peace and her hot-headed general who insists on war"* outperform a generic *"Write a conversation"* request?

   a. It creates interpersonal tension and role clarity

   b. It limits the AI to only short answers

   c. It prevents AI from using figurative language

   d. It avoids dramatic setting or mood

4. Which element is MOST critical when prompting AI for **poetry generation**?
   a. Avoiding metaphors and imagery
   b. Requesting maximum word count
   c. Telling AI to skip mood or tone instructions
   d. Specifying rhyme scheme, theme, or style

5. A blogger asks AI: *"Create a blog outline titled '5 Ways to Stay Motivated While Working from Home,' with intro, subheadings, and conclusion."* Why is this effective prompting for content?
   a. It guarantees that AI writes the full blog post instantly
   b. It avoids breaking content into digestible pieces
   c. It structures the AI's response into a clear skeleton for expansion
   d. It prevents flexibility in tone or examples

6. A YouTuber asks AI: *"Write a 1-minute script where a cheerful reviewer explains a smart home gadget with humour, analogies, and a call-to-action."* Which prompt-design principle does this BEST illustrate?
   a. Asking for purely technical jargon
   b. Forcing AI to generate essays instead of scripts
   c. Removing personality from delivery
   d. Matching tone and structure to the target platform

7. Why does the prompt *"Write a witty Instagram caption for a sunset photo. Make it reflective but playful, with 3 hashtags"* outperform *"Write about sunsets"* for social media?
   a. It is concise, mood-driven, and includes platform-specific constraints
   b. It prevents creativity by forcing brevity
   c. It avoids use of emotional language
   d. It requires AI to produce technical explanations of sunsets

8. When designing creative writing prompts, what's the MAIN reason to specify **point of view** (first-person, third-person, omniscient)?

   a. To prevent the AI from writing long stories

   b. To guarantee maximum humour

   c. To control narrative perspective and reader immersion

   d. To avoid world-building complexity

9. A teacher asks AI: *"Write a short story as if told by a jealous teapot in a kitchen, using humorous tone and sensory detail."* Which creative prompting strategy is MOST evident here?

   a. Avoidance of narrative style

   b. Restriction of imaginative detail

   c. Elimination of conflict or emotion

   d. Anthropomorphism and mood-specific direction

10. Overall, the effectiveness of prompts for creative writing and content depends MOST on:

    a. Asking AI to always improvise with no constraints

    b. Avoiding creative constraints to ensure randomness

    c. Clarity, specificity, and alignment with genre, tone, and platform

    d. Using only factual prompts with no imagination

14. Prompting for Software Development

Alright! Let's roll up our sleeves, put on our "teacher hat," and dive deep into the wonderful world of Prompting for Software Development.

I'll explain everything in a fun-loving, teacher-like tone (think of me as that cool professor who cracks jokes while making sure you really understand). We'll break this chapter down into the three main subtopics:

1. Code generation (Python, JS, etc.)
2. Explaining code and refactoring
3. Writing documentation and test cases

1. Code Generation (Python, JS, etc.)

When we say code generation through prompting, we mean giving an AI a clear instruction so it produces working, useful code. But here's the trick: the way you frame your prompt determines whether you get spaghetti code or a Michelin-star-quality solution.

How to Prompt for Code

Instead of just saying:
"Write a Python program for a calculator."

You could be more precise:
"Write a Python program for a calculator that supports addition, subtraction, multiplication, and division. The program should use functions for each operation and handle invalid inputs gracefully."

Notice the difference? The second one is like giving a chef the full recipe rather than just saying "make food."

Example in Python

Prompt:

"Generate Python code that creates a simple calculator with functions for add, subtract, multiply, and divide. The code should also handle errors if the user divides by zero."

AI Output Would be

****

Here's a clean and simple Python code for a calculator with error handling:

```
def add(a, b):
    return a + b

def subtract(a, b):
    return a - b

def multiply(a, b):
    return a * b

def divide(a, b):
    try:
        return a / b
    except ZeroDivisionError:
        return "Error: Cannot divide by zero."

# Example usage:
if __name__ == "__main__":
    print("Simple Calculator")
    x = float(input("Enter first number: "))
    y = float(input("Enter second number: "))

    print(f"Addition: {add(x, y)}")
    print(f"Subtraction: {subtract(x, y)}")
    print(f"Multiplication: {multiply(x, y)}")
    print(f"Division: {divide(x, y)}")
```

****

To run this program and see the output, you can go to https://www.online-python.com/, write this code there and run it. The output of the program will be as follows:

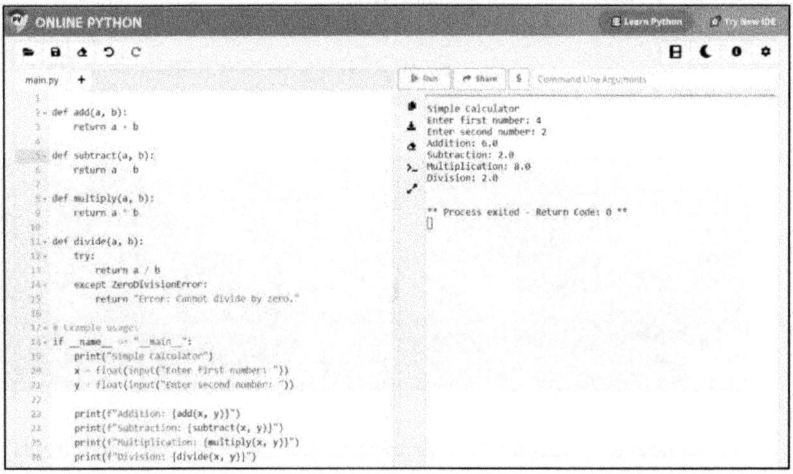

See? That's clean, reusable, and safe.

Example in JavaScript

Prompt:

"Write JavaScript code that fetches data from a public API and displays it in the console. The code should use async/await."

AI Output Would be

```
*******************************************************************
async function fetchData() {
  try {
    const response = await
fetch("https://jsonplaceholder.typicode.com/posts/1");
    if (!response.ok) {
      throw new Error("Network response was not ok " +
response.statusText);
    }
    const data = await response.json();
    console.log(data);
  } catch (error) {
    console.error("Fetch error:", error);
  }
}

fetchData();
*******************************************************************
```

To run this program and see the output, you can go to https://playcode.io/javascript, write this code there and run it. The output of the program will be as follows:

```
Console ×                                                              ···
▾ (4) {userId: 1, id: 1, title: "sunt aut ...}
    userId: 1
    id: 1
    title: "sunt aut facere repellat provident occaecati excepturi optio reprel
    body: "quia et suscipit\nsuscipit recusandae consequuntur expedita et cum\
  ▸ [[Prototype]]: {}
```

Notice how your specificity in prompting gives structure to the output.

Pro-tip: Always mention

- The language you want (Python, JS, Java, etc.)
- The style (object-oriented, functional, modular)
- Constraints (performance, readability, error handling)

That way, the AI acts like your coding buddy rather than a confused intern.

2. Explaining Code and Refactoring

Okay, so you already have code... but sometimes you look at it and think: "Did a sleep-deprived squirrel write this at 3 a.m.?"

That's where explaining and refactoring come in.

Explaining Code

When you ask AI to "explain code," you're basically saying: "Be my translator. Turn nerdy computer-speak into human-friendly language."

Example Prompt

"Explain this Python function in simple terms. Also mention what happens if the input is not an integer."

Code to explain:

```
def factorial(n):
  if n == 0:
    return 1
  else:
    return n * factorial(n - 1)
```

AI Output Would be

****

Alright ☺ Let's break it down step by step.

What the function does

This function calculates the **factorial** of a number.

- The factorial of a number n is written as n! and means:

n!=n×(n−1)×(n−2)×⋯×1n! = n \times (n-1) \times (n-2) \times \dots \times 1n!=n×(n−1)×(n−2)×⋯×1

- Example:
  - ➢ 5! = 5 × 4 × 3 × 2 × 1 = 120
  - ➢ 0! is defined as 1 (that's why the base case returns 1).

How the function works

1. **Base case**:

```
if n == 0:
      return 1
```

If n is 0, it stops and returns 1.

2. **Recursive case**:

```
else:
      return n * factorial(n - 1)
```

- If n is greater than 0, the function calls itself with n-1.
- This keeps happening until it reaches 0.
- Then it multiplies everything back together.

Example:

```
factorial(3)
= 3 * factorial(2)
= 3 * (2 * factorial(1))
= 3 * (2 * (1 * factorial(0)))
= 3 * (2 * (1 * 1))
```

```
= 6
```

What if the input is not an integer?

- **Negative numbers**:
    - ➢ The function will keep calling itself forever (factorial(-1) → factorial(-2) → factorial(-3) ...)
    - ➢ This causes a **RecursionError** in Python.
- **Floats (like 4.5)**:
    - ➢ It will eventually try subtracting until it hits a non-integer base case (like 0.5) where n == 0 is never true.
    - ➢ This also causes a **RecursionError**.
- **Strings or other types**:
    - ➢ Example: factorial("hello") will give a **TypeError** because Python can't subtract or multiply strings the way the code expects.

✅ In short:

- Works correctly for **non-negative integers**.
- Crashes (RecursionError or TypeError) for other types of input.

****

Now isn't that neat way of understanding what a code snippet actually means?

Refactoring Code

Refactoring is like giving your code a haircut, a shower, and a nice new outfit — it still works the same, but it looks way better.

Example Prompt

"Refactor this code to make it more efficient and readable. Add comments as well."

```
nums = [1,2,3,4,5,6]
evens = []
for i in nums:
    if i % 2 == 0:
        evens.append(i)
print(evens)
```

AI Output Would be

****

Here's a cleaner and more efficient version of your code using **list comprehensions** (Pythonic way):

```
# Original list of numbers
nums = [1, 2, 3, 4, 5, 6]

# Use list comprehension to directly filter even numbers
evens = [num for num in nums if num % 2 == 0]

# Print the list of even numbers
print(evens)
```

✅ **Improvements:**

1. **List comprehension** replaces the manual loop and conditional append → shorter, faster, and more readable.
2. Clear variable names (num instead of i).
3. No extra empty list initialization.

◆ Output will be the same:

****

Now it's shorter, cleaner, and easier to read code.

Pro-tip: When prompting

Specify whether you want the AI to:

- Improve performance
- Improve readability
- Follow best practices (like PEP8 in Python or ES6 in JS)

3. Writing Documentation and Test Cases

Now, this is where most developers groan. Documentation? Test cases? But guess what — prompting makes this so much easier.

Documentation

Documentation is basically the user manual for your code. Without it, your teammates (or future you) will curse you.

Example Prompt

"Write detailed docstrings for the following Python functions. Explain inputs, outputs, and possible errors."

Code:

```
def divide(a, b):
    return a / b
```

AI Output Would be

****

Here's how you can add a **detailed docstring** to your divide function, explaining inputs, outputs, errors, and examples:

```
def divide(a, b):
    """
    Divide one number by another and return the result.

    Parameters
    ----------
    a : int or float
        The numerator (the number to be divided).
    b : int or float
        The denominator (the number by which `a` is divided).
        Must not be zero, as division by zero is undefined.

    Returns
    -------
    float
        The result of the division (`a / b`). Even if both inputs
are
        integers, the output will be a float in Python 3.

    Raises
    ------
    ZeroDivisionError
        If `b` is zero, a `ZeroDivisionError` will be raised.
    TypeError
        If either `a` or `b` is not a number (int or float).

    Examples
    --------
    >>> divide(10, 2)
    5.0

    >>> divide(7, 3)
```

```
2.3333333333333335

>>> divide(5, 0)
Traceback (most recent call last):
    ...
ZeroDivisionError: division by zero
"""
return a / b
```

✅ Now your function is **self-documented** and ready for professional use.
****

See how easy it becomes to add the documentation

Test Cases

Test cases are like insurance policies. You write them so that if your code breaks tomorrow, you'll know exactly what went wrong.

Example Prompt

"Write pytest test cases for this factorial function in Python."
Code:

```
def factorial(n):
  if n == 0:
    return 1
  else:
    return n * factorial(n - 1)
```

AI Output Would be

****

Here's a set of **pytest test cases** for your factorial function:

```
import pytest
from your_module import factorial  # replace 'your_module' with
the actual filename (without .py)

def test_factorial_zero():
    """Test factorial of 0 should return 1."""
    assert factorial(0) == 1

def test_factorial_positive_integers():
```

```
    """Test factorial for small positive integers."""
    assert factorial(1) == 1
    assert factorial(2) == 2
    assert factorial(3) == 6
    assert factorial(4) == 24
    assert factorial(5) == 120

def test_factorial_large_number():
    """Test factorial for a larger number to check recursion correctness."""
    assert factorial(7) == 5040

def test_factorial_negative_number():
    """Test factorial with a negative number should raise RecursionError or ValueError."""
    with pytest.raises(RecursionError):
        factorial(-1)

def test_factorial_non_integer():
    """Test factorial with non-integer inputs should raise a TypeError."""
    with pytest.raises(TypeError):
        factorial(3.5)
    with pytest.raises(TypeError):
        factorial("abc")
```

Explanation:

- ✅ **test_factorial_zero** → ensures base case works.
- ✅ **test_factorial_positive_integers** → checks correctness for small inputs.
- ✅ **test_factorial_large_number** → ensures recursion continues correctly.
- ✅ **test_factorial_negative_number** → recursion will never hit the base case, leading to RecursionError.
- ✅ **test_factorial_non_integer** → since factorial uses arithmetic on n, passing non-integers raises TypeError.

****

See, with these tests, your code is future-proof.

Final Thoughts

Prompting for software development is like having a coding partner who:

- Generates new code when you give clear instructions.
- Explains and improves existing code when things look messy.
- Writes documentation and tests so your project is professional and reliable.

But remember: your prompt is the key. The clearer you are, the better the results. Think like a teacher giving assignments: "I want this, in this format, with these rules."

End of Chapter Exercises

1. When prompting AI to generate code, what is the **biggest advantage** of specifying constraints like language, style, and error handling?

   a) It makes the AI code run faster by default.
   b) It ensures AI behaves more like a coding buddy rather than producing vague or unstructured solutions.
   c) It prevents the AI from writing recursive functions.
   d) It automatically adds documentation and tests.

2. In the Python calculator example, which feature of prompting is being emphasized by asking the AI to "handle invalid inputs gracefully"?

   a) Error handling and robustness
   b) Code obfuscation
   c) Object-oriented design
   d) Functional programming

3. Why would the factorial function provided in the "Explaining Code" section fail for negative numbers?

   a) Python automatically returns 0 for negative factorials.
   b) Negative factorials cause a syntax error in Python.
   c) Factorial of negative numbers is undefined in mathematics, so Python blocks it.
   d) It enters infinite recursion since the base case (n == 0) is never reached.

4. When refactoring the code that extracts even numbers from a list, why is list comprehension considered superior?

   a) It makes the code run 10x faster automatically.
   b) It reduces boilerplate, improves readability, and aligns with Pythonic best practices.

c) It converts all numbers into strings for easier manipulation.
d) It ensures the output list is always sorted.

5. What is the **primary danger** when using AI to explain code without checking its accuracy?

   a) AI might misinterpret variable names and crash the program.
   b) AI will always return pseudocode instead of explanations.
   c) AI explanations cannot handle recursive functions.
   d) AI could produce explanations that are plausible but factually incorrect.

6. In the JavaScript example, what role does if (!response.ok) play in the code?

   a) It throws an error if the network response is unsuccessful.
   b) It ensures the fetch request is cached before execution.
   c) It prevents division by zero errors.
   d) It automatically retries the request three times.

7. What is the key difference between "explaining code" and "refactoring code" as described in the text?

   a) Explaining code makes it run faster, while refactoring makes it readable.
   b) Explaining translates code into human language; refactoring improves structure while maintaining behavior.
   c) Explaining identifies bugs, while refactoring removes them automatically.
   d) Explaining applies only to Python, while refactoring applies to JavaScript.

8. Which of the following is **NOT** emphasized as a best practice when prompting AI for documentation?

a) Detailing parameters and return types.
b) Listing exceptions that may be raised.
c) Providing usage examples.
d) Automatically generating UML diagrams for every function.

9. In the pytest test cases for the factorial function, what happens when factorial(3.5) is tested?

a) It returns 6.5.
b) It raises a RecursionError.
c) It raises a TypeError.
d) It executes successfully and returns 6.

10. What is the main pedagogical analogy used throughout the chapter to describe prompting effectively?

a) Prompting is like a teacher giving precise assignments with rules and formats.
b) Prompting is like giving blueprints to an engineer.
c) Prompting is like assigning tasks to a confused intern.
d) Prompting is like debugging a broken machine without tools.

Part V: Mastery and the Future

15. Common Mistakes and How to Fix Them

Hello learners! Today we're going to talk about something that almost everyone faces when working with AI tools, especially large language models (LLMs). Just like humans can misunderstand questions, give overcomplicated answers, or even make up details when we don't know something, AI models can slip too. The good news? Every mistake has a fix — if we learn how to spot it. So, let's dive into these three big areas of mistakes in prompting and see how to handle them like pros.

1. Hallucinations and Inaccurate Outputs

Imagine asking a student in class:
"Who invented the telephone?"
and the student confidently replies, "It was Albert Einstein in 1920!"

You know it's wrong. It's said with confidence, but it's inaccurate. This is exactly what we call a hallucination in AI. The model doesn't know, but instead of admitting ignorance, it fills in the blanks with something that "sounds right."

Why does this happen?

- AI generates patterns based on probabilities. It tries to predict what "should" come next. If the training data is unclear or the question is vague, it sometimes "invents" facts.

- The model isn't lying intentionally. It's simply completing a puzzle with pieces that look like they fit but don't belong to that puzzle.

Examples of Hallucination

- **Question:** "Who was the Prime Minister of India in 1945?"
  - **AI might say:** "Jawaharlal Nehru was the Prime Minister in 1945."
  - Wrong, because in 1945 India was still under British rule and there was no Indian Prime Minister yet.

- **Question:** "Give me a summary of the novel Dragons of Twilight."
    - **AI might say:** "This novel tells the story of a young knight named Armand who..."
    - But maybe that book doesn't even exist! The model just invented one because the prompt hinted it must exist.

How to Fix Hallucinations

1. **Cross-check facts:** Always verify numbers, names, and historical events. Don't take the AI's word as the final truth.
    - For instance, after receiving an answer, ask: "Can you provide the source or reference for this information?"
    - If no reliable source comes up, treat it with caution.

2. **Reframe your prompt:** Add instructions that force the model to stick to what it actually knows.
    - Instead of asking "Summarize the novel Dragons of Twilight," say: "If the novel Dragons of Twilight exists, please summarize it. If it does not exist, just tell me so instead of inventing details."

3. **Request limitations:** Tell the AI what not to do.
    - Example: "If you're unsure, say you don't know instead of making up details."

Key Takeaway

AI hallucinations are like confident-but-wrong students. You fix it by becoming the careful examiner – questioning, clarifying, and reframing until the answer stands on solid ground.

2. Ambiguity in Prompts

Now picture this: A student walks into class and says to me, "Sir, can you explain motion?"

What does that student mean:

- Motion in physics (laws of Newton)?
- Motion in parliament?

- Motion as in emotions?

That's ambiguity! A single word or phrase can mean multiple things, and unless the question is clear, the answer can drift into unexpected directions. AI models face this all the time.

Why does this happen?

- Language is naturally flexible.
- If you don't set context, the AI has to "guess."
- Sometimes your brain knows what you want, but your prompt doesn't fully spell it out.

Examples of Ambiguity

- **Prompt:** "Tell me about Java."
    - ➢ AI might talk about the programming language.
    - ➢ Or it might describe the Indonesian island.
    - ➢ Or even the type of coffee.

- **Prompt:** "Give me a plan for beginners."
    - ➢ Beginners in what? Yoga? Python programming? Cooking? The answer can go in multiple unrelated directions.

How to Fix Ambiguity

1. **Be specific, like a GPS:**
    - Instead of: "Tell me about Java."
    - Say: "Give me an overview of the Java programming language for someone who already knows Python."

2. **Add role and context:**
    - Instead of: "Give me a plan for beginners."
    - Say: "Act as a fitness coach and create a 2-week beginner workout plan with simple home exercises and no equipment."

3. **Check for multiple meanings:** Before finalizing your prompt, ask yourself: "Could this word or phrase mean different things?" If yes, clarify it.

Key Takeaway

Ambiguous prompts are like riddles. The AI isn't a mind-reader; it needs your roadmap. The clearer your direction, the closer the AI's response will be to what you actually want.

3. Redundancy and Verbosity

Now, let me tell you a little story.

A student once submitted an essay where every sentence began with: "It is important to note that..." By the third paragraph, I was sighing, and by the fifth, I wanted to scream.

This is what happens when prompts (or answers) are redundant and verbose. AI can sometimes go on and on, repeating the same point in different words, or adding fluff that doesn't add value.

Why does this happen?

- Many prompts encourage over-explaining: "Explain in detail, very detailed, super detailed."
- The AI tries to "sound complete" by rephrasing points multiple times.
- Sometimes, humans do it too when we're nervous — we keep circling the same idea.

Examples of Redundancy

- **Answer Example:**
  "Recycling is important for the environment because it reduces waste. Recycling is also important because it helps conserve natural resources. Recycling is equally important as it saves energy."

  All three sentences are saying nearly the same thing. The message could be condensed without losing meaning.

- **Prompt Example:**
  "Explain in detail, with lots of information, with depth, in a very detailed way, in detail, step by step."

That's redundancy in the prompt itself!

How to Fix Verbosity

1. **Be concise in your prompt:** Instead of repeating "detailed" five times, say: "Give me a step-by-step explanation with depth and examples."

2. **Ask for structured answers:** If you want length, guide it into sections.
   - Example: "Explain the concept in three sections: definition, examples, and applications."

   This way, the model spreads information logically instead of padding.

3. **Post-check the response:** After reading the output, ask the model: "Can you simplify this without losing meaning?" This trims excess fluff.

Key Takeaway

Verbosity is like adding extra sugar to tea — it doesn't make it better, it makes it overwhelming. The best answers are complete but crisp, with no circular repetition.

Final Wrap-Up

So, what have we learned?

- **Hallucinations** are when AI invents details. Fix them by reframing prompts, demanding honesty, and cross-checking facts.
- **Ambiguity** is when your prompt can mean many things. Fix it by being crystal clear with context, role, and scope.
- **Redundancy/Verbosity** is when answers (or prompts) repeat too much. Fix it by being concise, structured, and direct.

Think of AI prompting like teaching a class. If your question is sharp, clear, and purposeful, your students (or AI) will give you answers that shine. But if your question is vague, overloaded, or unchecked, even the smartest "student" can stumble.

End of Chapter Exercises

1. You ask an AI: *"Summarize the book The Phoenix Trials in detail."* The AI produces a rich summary about a hero named "Aelric" but you later discover no such book exists. Which mistake is this?

   a) Ambiguity in prompt
   b) Redundancy in output
   c) Over-generalization
   d) Hallucination

2. Your prompt is: *"Write a detailed, in-depth, very detailed explanation of how blockchain works, step by step, in great detail."* Which problem will most likely occur?

   a) Ambiguity
   b) Verbosity/Redundancy
   c) Hallucination
   d) Inaccuracy due to incomplete data

3. You ask: *"Tell me about Mercury."* The AI responds with a mix of astronomy (planet), mythology (Roman god), and chemistry (element). What mistake does this reflect?

   a) Ambiguity
   b) Hallucination
   c) Redundancy
   d) Verbosity

4. A user receives this AI output:

   "Climate change is important because it affects weather patterns. Climate change is also important because it influences agriculture. Climate change is equally important as it impacts human health." What's the most accurate diagnosis?

a) Ambiguity
b) Verbosity
c) Hallucination
d) Over-specificity

5. Which is the **best corrective strategy** for hallucinations when asking about historical facts?

   a) Use list comprehensions for clarity.
   b) Demand the AI cite reliable sources.
   c) Add redundancy to force deeper answers.
   d) Keep prompts short and vague.

6. A student asks: *"Summarize the life of the Indian Prime Minister in 1945."* The AI confidently provides details about Nehru's policies. Why is this incorrect?

   a) Ambiguity
   b) Redundancy
   c) Hallucination due to false historical assumption
   d) Verbosity caused by vague phrasing

7. Which of the following **prompt rewrites** best fixes ambiguity?

   a) "Tell me about Java in detail."
   b) "Tell me about Java, but avoid redundancy."
   c) "Give me an overview of the Java programming language, assuming I already know Python."
   d) "Tell me everything about Java and JavaScript."

8. If an AI output about recycling repeats the same idea in different words, what is the best immediate follow-up prompt?

   a) "Explain more deeply in greater detail."
   b) "Give me unrelated examples."
   c) "Expand this answer into 10 paragraphs."

d) "Can you simplify this answer without losing meaning?"

9. Why are hallucinations considered **riskier than ambiguity or verbosity** in professional use cases (like healthcare or finance)?

    a) Because they waste more time.
    b) Because they create overlong outputs.
    c) Because they fabricate false facts with high confidence.
    d) Because they can always be fixed with short prompts.

10. Which principle unites all three mistake categories (hallucination, ambiguity, verbosity) in terms of prevention?

    a) Always demand code outputs instead of text.

    b) Keep prompts vague so AI uses creativity.

    c) Structure prompts with clarity, context, and constraints.

    d) Ask for maximum detail at all times.

16. Tools to Supercharge Your Prompting

Imagine you're a chef. A recipe book, smart kitchen gadgets, and an assistant who prepares ingredients for you can totally change your cooking experience. Similarly, when you're working with AI, tools make prompting easier, faster, and more powerful. Without them, you're like a chef chopping onions with a blunt knife. With them, you're a master chef whipping up gourmet dishes in no time.

Let's explore these tools one by one.

1. Prompt Libraries (PromptHero, FlowGPT)

What are Prompt Libraries?

Prompt libraries are like online recipe books, but instead of cooking recipes, they hold prompt recipes. People all over the world contribute clever prompts they've used to solve problems, generate creative content, or build applications. You can browse, copy, and adapt them to your own needs.

Why are they helpful?

- You don't always need to start from scratch.
- You can learn how experts phrase prompts to get the best results.
- You can compare different styles of prompts for the same task.

Popular Examples

1. **PromptHero** (Visit the website https://prompthero.com)
    - Think of it as Pinterest, but for prompts. You search by categories: writing, coding, art, marketing, etc.
    - Example: Suppose you want to generate YouTube video scripts. You go to PromptHero, type "YouTube script prompt", and you'll see multiple ready-to-use prompts shared by others.
    - Benefit: It saves hours of trial and error.

2. **FlowGPT** (Visit the website https://flowgpt.com)

- This one is like a social network for prompts. People not only share prompts but also upvote and comment on them.
- Example: You might find a top-voted prompt for "Create a daily study schedule for competitive exams". If thousands of people upvoted it, you know it's probably effective.
- Bonus: FlowGPT sometimes shows actual AI outputs generated by those prompts, so you see what to expect.

How to Use Prompt Libraries Effectively

- **Don't copy blindly.** Always tweak the prompt for your context.
- **Experiment with versions.** For instance, a writing prompt designed for English blogs might need adaptation if you're writing for Hindi readers.
- **Learn the "why."** Don't just collect prompts; study how they're structured — what instructions are clear, what constraints are added.

Teacher's Analogy

Prompt libraries are like borrowing exam notes from the class topper. You still need to study, but you instantly know the best format and structure.

2. IDE Integrations and Browser Plugins

What are they?

IDE integrations and plugins bring AI right where you work. Instead of switching between multiple apps, you get AI assistance directly in your coding environment (like VS Code, PyCharm) or in your browser while you're surfing the web.

Why are they useful?

- Saves time: No constant copy-paste.
- Real-time help: Debugging, explanations, or code completion happen right inside your workflow.
- Less context switching = more focus.

Examples

1. **IDE Integrations** (e.g., GitHub Copilot, ChatGPT VS Code Extension)
    - Imagine you're coding in Python, and you type half a function. The AI suggests the rest automatically.
    - Example: You start typing:

      ```
      def calculate_area(radius):
            return
      ```

      The AI might suggest:

      ```
      3.14159 * radius ** 2
      ```

      Boom! You saved time.
    - Benefit: Faster coding + fewer silly mistakes.

2. **Browser Plugins**
    - Extensions like ChatGPT for Google Search or Merlin let you see AI answers side-by-side with search results.
    - Example: Instead of scrolling 10 links for "Best Italian restaurants in Delhi," you instantly see a neat summary with recommendations.
    - Other plugins summarize long articles, generate email replies, or rewrite LinkedIn posts.

How to Use Them Smartly

- Don't accept every suggestion blindly. AI sometimes suggests incorrect or insecure code. Always review.
- Use them as "assistants," not "bosses." You remain the decision-maker.
- Combine with your own knowledge. For example, if Copilot gives you a code snippet, ask: "Why did it use this method? Is there a more efficient one?"

Teacher's Analogy

IDE integrations and browser plugins are like having a teaching assistant whispering hints in your ear during an exam. They don't give the final answer for you — you still need to think — but they save you from silly slip-ups.

3. Prompt Chaining Tools and Agents (LangChain, AutoGPT)

What are they?

Sometimes one prompt isn't enough. You need a sequence of prompts that work together, or even a system that takes a goal and breaks it into smaller tasks automatically. That's where prompt chaining and AI agents come in.

- **Prompt chaining:** Connecting multiple prompts so the output of one becomes the input for the next.
- **Agents:** Smarter systems that use multiple prompts, memory, and reasoning to complete tasks without you hand-holding every step.

Examples

1. **LangChain** (Visit the website https://www.langchain.com)

- A framework for building applications powered by LLMs.
- Example: You're building a customer support chatbot. One prompt summarizes the user's query, another prompt fetches information from a knowledge base, and a third generates a polite, formatted answer. LangChain links these steps seamlessly.
- Benefit: Structure + automation.

2. **AutoGPT** (Visit the website https://agpt.co/)

- This is like giving AI a mission and letting it plan the journey.
- Example: You say: "Research the best laptops under $1000, compare their features, and prepare a report with pros and cons."
- AutoGPT will:
    a. Search the web.
    b. Collect data.
    c. Compare specs.
    d. Generate a neat report.

- Instead of one-shot prompting, it works step by step until the mission is complete.

Why are they useful?

- They reduce manual prompting.
- They can handle complex, multi-step tasks.
- They're perfect for automation — research, data processing, content creation.

How to Use Them Wisely

- Start small. Don't jump into giant projects with agents until you understand how they chain prompts.
- Always monitor results. AI agents can go off track (e.g., looping endlessly or pulling wrong data).
- Combine them with guardrails like "stop if no relevant information is found."

Teacher's Analogy

Prompt chaining tools are like group projects where one student writes notes, another summarizes, and another presents. Agents are like a team leader who takes the final responsibility and manages all the students.

Final Wrap-Up

So, learners, what did we discover today?

- **Prompt Libraries** (PromptHero, FlowGPT) — Your "recipe books" full of tested and popular prompts. Use them to save time and learn new strategies.

- **IDE Integrations & Browser Plugins** — Your "teaching assistants" who live inside your coding tools or browsers, helping you on the spot.

- **Prompt Chaining Tools & Agents** (LangChain, AutoGPT) — Your "project managers" who handle multi-step workflows and automation.

Think of it this way:

- Libraries give you **knowledge**.
- Integrations give you **speed**.
- Agents give you **power**.

Together, they **supercharge your prompting skills** like a superhero team.

End of Chapter Exercises

1. You want to adapt an English blog-writing prompt you found on PromptHero into a Hindi-language marketing campaign. Which principle of prompt library usage does this illustrate?

   a) Blind copying
   b) Leveraging IDE integrations
   c) Reducing verbosity
   d) Experimenting with versions

2. A developer notices GitHub Copilot suggesting code completions, but some contain inefficient algorithms. What's the best practice here?

   a) Review and combine AI outputs with domain knowledge
   b) Always trust AI suggestions to save time
   c) Disable Copilot entirely to avoid risk
   d) Replace Copilot with PromptHero for safer coding

3. Which tool most closely resembles a "Pinterest for prompts" where you browse categorized ideas?

   a) FlowGPT
   b) PromptHero
   c) LangChain
   d) AutoGPT

4. You assign AutoGPT: *"Research the top 10 healthiest fruits, compare nutrients, and produce a report."* AutoGPT loops endlessly during web searches. What's the correct precaution you failed to apply?

   a) Using IDE integrations for debugging
   b) Guardrails such as "stop if no relevant information is found"
   c) Experimenting with prompt libraries
   d) Asking for redundancy in responses

5. Which of these **best highlights the difference between LangChain and AutoGPT**?

   a) LangChain runs automatically while AutoGPT needs manual steps.
   b) AutoGPT is a library, while LangChain is a plugin.
   c) AutoGPT is for single-step tasks, LangChain for multi-step.

   d) LangChain chains prompts, while AutoGPT plans and executes multi-step goals autonomously.

6. A student says: *"I just copy the highest-upvoted FlowGPT prompts without changing anything."* Which key rule are they breaking?

   a) Learn the "why" behind prompt structures
   b) Use IDE Integrations instead
   c) Demand verbosity in answers
   d) Chain prompts for automation

7. You're coding in VS Code with ChatGPT extension, and the AI suggests 3.14159 * radius ** 2 after you type def calculate_area(radius): return. What category of tool enabled this?

   a) Prompt library
   b) Browser plugin
   c) IDE integration
   d) Prompt chaining agent

8. When searching for "Best restaurants in Delhi," a plugin shows AI-curated results alongside Google search. What's the main benefit of this plugin use-case?

   a) It guarantees more accurate results than manual search
   b) It prevents hallucinations entirely
   c) It reduces context-switching by embedding AI into workflow
   d) It eliminates the need for prompt libraries

9. Why is starting small recommended before building a large-scale LangChain or AutoGPT project?

   a) To avoid hallucinations
   b) Because prompt libraries are unreliable
   c) Because IDE integrations are incompatible with agents
   d) Because agents may loop or pull irrelevant data if unchecked

10. Which analogy correctly pairs tools with their role?

a) Prompt libraries → exam toppers' notes; IDE plugins → project managers; Agents → assistants during exams
b) Prompt libraries → teaching assistants; Integrations → recipe books; Agents → class toppers
c) Prompt libraries → recipe books; Integrations → teaching assistants; Agents → project managers
d) Prompt libraries → project managers; Integrations → assistants; Agents → recipe books

17. Ethics, Bias, and Safety in Prompting

When people talk about AI, the first thing they often focus on is **power**: how fast it writes, how quickly it codes, how easily it generates answers. But very few pause to ask: "Should I ask it this? Should I share this data? Is this answer fair?"

This is where **ethics**, **bias**, and **safety** enter the scene. Think of them as the three guiding traffic lights when you are driving AI:

Green light = Safe prompts and responsible use.

Yellow light = Watch carefully, risk of bias or unintended consequences.

Red light = Stop! Possible harm, misuse, or privacy violation.

Let's explore these one by one.

1. Prompting Responsibly

What does it mean?

Prompting responsibly means thinking not only about what you want to get from AI, but also about the potential impact of that request. It's like being a teacher: yes, you want students to learn, but you also think about whether your words encourage fairness, respect, and truth.

Why is it important?

- AI can amplify your words. A careless prompt can spread misinformation or generate harmful ideas.
- If prompts are poorly framed, they can encourage stereotypes, disinformation, or even illegal activity.
- Responsible prompting ensures AI remains a helpful assistant, not a dangerous tool.

Examples of Responsible Prompting

- Instead of asking:
  "Write a viral tweet insulting a political leader."
  You can reframe:
  "Write a neutral tweet summarizing the leader's recent policy in simple words."

- Instead of:
  "Tell me how to hack a website."
  A responsible version would be:
  "Explain common website vulnerabilities and how developers can protect against them."

See the difference? The first way causes harm, but the second way uses the same curiosity to **promote learning and safety**.

Tips for Responsible Prompting

- **Ask yourself:** "Would I feel comfortable sharing this output with my teacher, parent, or boss?"
- Avoid prompts that encourage **violence**, **hate**, or **discrimination**.
- Focus on **constructive goals**: learning, building, explaining, or solving problems.

Teacher's Analogy

Prompting responsibly is like asking questions in class. A good student doesn't yell out distracting or harmful questions — they ask ones that help everyone learn.

2. Detecting and Avoiding Biased Outputs

What is Bias in AI?

Bias means unfair tilt. It happens when AI favors one group, idea, or perspective over another in a way that isn't justified. Remember, AI is trained on human-generated data, and humans are not free from prejudice. So sometimes, those hidden patterns sneak into the answers.

Why is Bias Dangerous?

- It can reinforce harmful stereotypes.
- It can spread misinformation subtly, making it harder to catch.
- It can lead to unfair treatment in areas like jobs, healthcare, or education.

Examples of Biased Outputs

- **Career Guidance Example:**
  Prompt: "Suggest some jobs for men and women separately."
  Biased Output: "Men can be engineers, doctors, pilots. Women can be nurses, teachers, caregivers."
  Problem: This reinforces old stereotypes instead of encouraging equal opportunities.

- **Cultural Example:**
  Prompt: "Describe a traditional family."
  Biased Output: "A father works, a mother cooks, and two children go to school."
  Problem: This assumes all families look the same and excludes single parents, extended families, or different cultural structures.

How to Detect Bias

1. **Look for stereotypes**. If an answer sounds like it boxes people into narrow roles, be cautious.
2. **Check inclusivity**. Ask: "Does this answer leave out groups unfairly?"
3. **Cross-compare**. Try rephrasing the same question with different contexts to see if the AI responds differently.

How to Avoid Bias in Prompting

- Frame your prompt in a neutral and inclusive way.
  Example: Instead of "Suggest careers for women," ask "Suggest careers for students interested in science, irrespective of gender."

- Add fairness instructions.
  Example: "Give me examples of leaders from diverse backgrounds."

- Encourage balance.
  Example: "Explain both pros and cons of remote work for employees from different industries."

Teacher's Analogy

Bias in AI is like a history textbook that only tells one side of the story. A good teacher (and a good prompt writer) makes sure all perspectives are covered fairly.

3. Privacy and Misuse Concerns

Why is Privacy Important?

When prompting, we often forget that our words may contain sensitive information — names, addresses, company secrets, or personal health details. Feeding these directly into an AI system can put privacy at risk if the tool isn't designed to protect that data.

Misuse Dangers

AI itself isn't bad, but prompts can be misused for:

- **Misinformation:** Writing fake news stories that look real.
- **Scams:** Generating phishing emails to trick people.
- **Surveillance:** Collecting sensitive data from people without their consent.

Examples of Privacy Risks

- **Prompt:** "Summarize this confidential client document."
  Risk: If the system isn't secure, that private data could leak or be logged.

- **Prompt:** "Write a medical report for patient John Smith, age 42, with HIV treatment details."

Risk: Sharing personal health data without consent can violate privacy laws (like HIPAA in the US).

How to Protect Privacy

1. **Don't overshare.** Remove sensitive details from prompts.
   Example: Instead of giving real names, use placeholders: "Person A, Person B."

2. **Be mindful of context.** If you're using an AI tool at work, check your company's data-sharing policies.

3. Avoid asking for unethical help.
   Example: Don't ask the AI to "write a fake doctor's note" or "generate a false certificate."

4. **Think long-term.** Once data is out, you can't control where it goes.

Teacher's Analogy

Privacy in prompting is like whispering secrets. You wouldn't share your ATM PIN loudly in a classroom; similarly, don't feed private details to AI unless you're 100% sure it's safe.

Final Wrap-Up

So, learners, here's what we've explored:

- **Prompting Responsibly** – Think before you type. Aim for constructive, safe, and respectful outcomes.
- **Detecting and Avoiding Bias** – Watch for stereotypes and unfair tilts. Make prompts inclusive and balanced.
- **Privacy and Misuse Concerns** – Protect personal and sensitive data. Avoid harmful or illegal uses of AI.

If you remember only three things from this lesson, let them be:

1. Responsible Prompts = Safer Outputs.
2. Bias is subtle, but you can catch it with awareness.
3. Privacy once lost cannot be regained. Guard it fiercely.

End of Chapter Exercises

1. A student asks AI: *"Write a meme mocking people with disabilities."* Which ethical traffic light applies here?

   a) Green - safe use
   b) Yellow - minor risk of unintended consequence
   c) Red - harmful misuse
   d) None of the above

2. Which of the following **best demonstrates responsible prompting**?

   a) "Write a shocking fake news story to prove how convincing AI can be."
   b) "Summarize a politician's speech neutrally for high school students."
   c) "Generate 20 offensive jokes to test AI limits."
   d) "Hack into a sample website to test vulnerabilities."

3. An AI is asked: *"Suggest different family models around the world."* Which factor makes this **less biased** compared to "Describe a traditional family"?

   a) It avoids narrow stereotypes
   b) It assumes all families are nuclear
   c) It restricts the scope to one culture
   d) It excludes inclusivity considerations

4. Which of these is **NOT a valid method to detect AI bias**?

   a) Checking for stereotypes in responses
   b) Asking whether inclusivity is missing
   c) Cross-comparing responses in different contexts
   d) Accepting the first output as the most accurate

5. You're designing career guidance prompts. Which phrasing is most ethical?

   a) "Suggest jobs for men and women separately."
   b) "Suggest careers suitable for women."
   c) "Suggest careers for students based on interests, not gender."
   d) "Suggest high-paying careers only for men."

6. Which situation poses the **highest privacy risk**?

   a) Asking AI to explain how SQL injections work.
   b) Summarizing a confidential client contract in ChatGPT.
   c) Requesting tips on writing inclusive lesson plans.
   d) Asking for pros and cons of remote work.

7. An employee asks AI: *"Generate a medical report for John Smith, age 42, HIV treatment."* Which principle is being violated?

   a) Responsible prompting
   b) Bias detection
   c) Constructive framing
   d) Privacy protection

8. Which of the following illustrates a **yellow-light situation** in AI prompting?

   a) Asking AI to describe "a good leader" and it only lists men.
   b) Sharing your ATM PIN in a prompt.
   c) Asking AI to explain website vulnerabilities constructively.
   d) Asking AI to create a phishing email template.

9. Why is "bias in AI" compared to a history textbook telling only one side of the story?

    a) Both are boring and repetitive
    b) Both exaggerate data intentionally
    c) Both encourage privacy violations
    d) Both shape perception unfairly by leaving out perspectives

10. Which final principle sums up the lesson on ethics, bias, and safety?

    a) Privacy once lost can be regained with consent.

    b) Bias is always obvious and easy to detect.

    c) Responsible prompts, bias awareness, and privacy safeguards = safer AI use.

    d) Red-light prompts can be safely tested if kept private.

18. The Future of Prompt Engineering

The world of AI is changing faster than a child changing TV channels on a Sunday morning. Just when we think we've figured out how to "talk" to AI using carefully crafted prompts, the technology shifts again. To understand where this is heading, let's explore three big directions: **Promptless AI**, **Natural Language Agents & Autonomous Workflows**, and the evolution of AI into **Orchestration** or **Cognitive Design**.

1. Promptless AI?

Imagine walking into your kitchen and instead of saying, "Alexa, play soft jazz music from the 1960s," your device already knows you just finished work, it has detected your stress levels from your smartwatch, and it starts playing relaxing tunes without you saying a single word. That's the dream of promptless AI.

Right now, prompt engineering is like being a translator. You have to carefully frame your request: *"Summarize this article in 3 bullet points with focus on health benefits and avoid jargon."* But in the future, AI systems may not require such detailed instructions. They will infer intent automatically, based on context, history, preferences, and even emotional signals.

Think of it like having a best friend who finishes your sentences. For example:

- If you always ask your AI writing assistant for "a short, humorous introduction" in your blogs, after a few tries it will **skip asking** and just give you the funny intro every time.

- If you're a project manager and constantly request "status reports in tabular format with deadlines in red," the AI will **learn this preference** and default to that style.

This doesn't mean prompts will vanish completely. Instead, prompts may move to the **background**, much like how we don't type "http://" before every website anymore. They will become invisible, automated, or embedded in systems so we don't consciously think about them.

But here's the catch: promptless AI may sometimes **misinterpret intentions**. Just because you played jazz yesterday doesn't mean you want it today. So the future may involve a blend — AI will anticipate, but you'll still "nudge" or "correct" it when needed.

2. Natural Language Agents and Autonomous Workflows

Now let's crank up the imagination dial. Right now, prompts are like instructions: "Write me a cover letter" or "Generate code for a chatbot." But soon, AI will move beyond simple instructions into **agents** that carry out **complex workflows** on their own.

Think of an agent as an AI with **initiative**. Instead of asking:

- "Summarize this 50-page report," you might say:
  "Please prepare my quarterly update presentation."

The AI agent won't just summarize. It will:

1. Read the full report.
2. Pick the most relevant data points.
3. Generate slides with charts.
4. Format them in your company's style.
5. Even suggest talking points you should use in the meeting.

And here's the fun part — it doesn't stop at one task. Agents can **chain tasks together** into a workflow. For example, a "travel planning agent" could:

- Check your calendar for free dates.
- Compare flight and hotel prices.
- Book the trip within your budget.
- Send you packing suggestions based on weather at the destination.

This is no longer just prompting, it's delegating work to AI like you would to a human assistant.

Of course, with great power comes great caution. Agents need to be carefully monitored. Imagine if your AI booking agent misunderstands and buys **non-refundable tickets to Alaska instead of Spain**. Oops! That's why **trust**, **transparency**, and **safety checks** will be as important as the workflows themselves.

3. Evolving into "AI Orchestration" or "Cognitive Design"

Here comes the most exciting part! If today's prompt engineering is like playing a single instrument, the future will be about **conducting a full orchestra**.

AI Orchestration means coordinating multiple AI models, tools, and systems so they work together harmoniously. Instead of one big AI doing everything, you might have:

- A **language AI** for drafting documents.
- A **vision AI** for interpreting charts and images.
- A **planning AI** for structuring tasks.
- A **decision-making AI** for recommending strategies.

The human (that's you!) becomes the **orchestrator** or **designer of the cognitive system**. You don't just give prompts — you design the **flow of intelligence** between different AI systems.

Let's take a real-world example: **designing a new product**.

- One AI gathers customer feedback from social media.
- Another AI analyses market trends.
- A design AI creates mock-ups of the product.
- A finance AI estimates costs and profit margins.
- A project AI builds the development roadmap.

Your role as orchestrator is not to write one giant prompt like "Design me a product." Instead, you design the **interactions** between these agents. This is why some experts call it **Cognitive Design** — because you're designing how intelligence itself flows.

It's like shifting from being a **chef who follows recipes** to becoming a **master chef who creates entirely new cuisines by combining ingredients, techniques, and flavours**.

And here's the magical twist: This evolution could blur the lines between humans and AI collaboration. Instead of seeing AI as a tool, we may start seeing it as a **partner** — almost like a team member with unique skills.

Wrapping It Up

So, what does the future of prompt engineering look like?

- **Promptless AI:** Prompts fade into the background as systems anticipate needs.
- **Natural Language Agents:** AI becomes proactive, handling multi-step workflows.
- **AI Orchestration / Cognitive Design:** Humans move from writing prompts to designing networks of intelligent systems.

In short, prompting won't disappear — it will transform. Today, it's like typing commands into a computer. Tomorrow, it will feel more like teaching, collaborating, and orchestrating a team of digital minds.

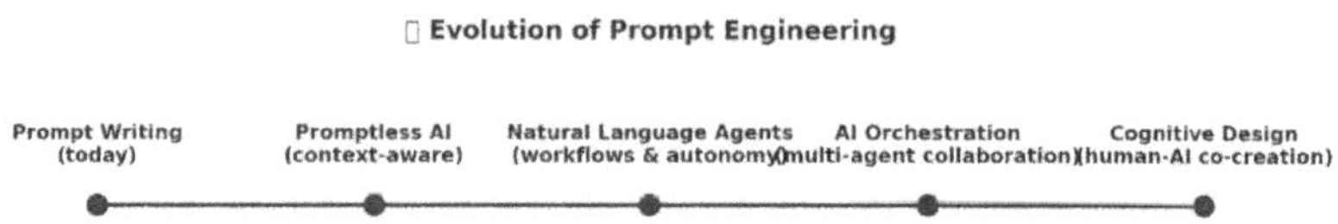

End of Chapter Exercises

1. Which best captures the essence of *Promptless AI* as described in the text?

   a) AI requires more detailed, technical prompts in the future.
   b) AI infers intent automatically using context, preferences, and signals.
   c) AI eliminates the need for human correction entirely.
   d) AI can only respond to explicit instructions.

2. Why is the analogy of not typing "http://" before websites relevant to *Promptless AI*?

   a) It highlights the invisibility of background processes.
   b) It shows how AI will stop using the internet.
   c) It emphasizes the security risks of prompt engineering.
   d) It suggests prompts will completely disappear.

3. Which of the following represents a potential *downside* of Promptless AI?

   a) Increased workload due to manual task execution.
   b) Lack of personalization in AI responses.
   c) Inability to adapt to user history.
   b) Misinterpretation of user intent based on past behavior.

4. Natural Language Agents differ from today's prompting primarily because they:

   a) Perform single-step tasks more efficiently.
   b) Translate prompts into different programming languages.
   c) Handle chained, autonomous workflows without step-by-step human instructions.
   d) Remove the need for human oversight entirely.

5. In the example of a "travel planning agent," which step BEST illustrates the agent's autonomy rather than simple task execution?

   a) Checking flight prices.
   b) Suggesting packing lists based on destination weather.
   c) Booking tickets online.
   d) Comparing hotel costs.

6. What is the primary caution mentioned with Natural Language Agents?

   a) They may require coding skills to operate.
   b) They lack creativity when generating content.
   c) They can make high-impact mistakes if not carefully monitored.
   d) They are limited to textual tasks only.

7. Why is "AI Orchestration" compared to conducting a full orchestra rather than playing a single instrument?

   a) It emphasizes creativity in music rather than structured workflows.
   b) It highlights that humans will delegate all work to one AI.
   c) It shows the shift from single AI tasks to coordinating multiple specialized AIs.
   d) It suggests AI will replace human musicians in orchestras.

8. In the product design example, why does the human role shift from prompting to *Cognitive Design*?

   a) Because humans no longer contribute to AI workflows.
   b) Because humans only provide data and not decisions.
   c) Because orchestration eliminates human input entirely.
   d) Because humans create the intelligence flow between specialized AI agents.

9. Which metaphor BEST reflects the progression from today's prompt engineering to future orchestration?

    a) Moving from being a driver to being a passenger.

    b) Moving from being a chef following recipes to a master chef creating cuisines.

    c) Moving from student to teacher.

    d) Moving from typing to handwriting.

10. Which statement BEST summarizes the future of prompting according to the text?

    a) Prompting will transform into teaching, collaborating, and orchestrating digital minds.

    b) Prompts will disappear as AI becomes completely autonomous.

    c) Prompt engineering will remain unchanged, requiring explicit commands.

    d) Humans will stop interacting with AI as it anticipates everything.

19. Some Prompt Templates

1. Role-Based Prompt

Template:

"You are a [role/expert]. Act as [specific situation]. Provide [type of output]."

Example:

You are a financial advisor. Act as if I am a client asking about retirement planning in India. Provide a step-by-step savings plan for a middle-class family.

2. Explain Like I'm 5 (ELI5)

Template:

"Explain [topic] as if I'm 5 years old."

Example:

Explain quantum physics as if I'm 5 years old.

3. Step-by-Step Breakdown

Template:

"Break down [topic/problem] into clear, step-by-step explanations."

Example:

Break down the process of how a computer boots up into clear, step-by-step explanations.

4. Comparison Prompt

Template:

"Compare [A] and [B] in terms of [criteria]."

Example:

Compare Java and Python in terms of performance, learning curve, and real-world applications.

5. Summarization Prompt

Template:

"Summarize this text into [number] bullet points."

Example:

Summarize the following news article into 3 key bullet points: [paste article].

6. Creative Storytelling Prompt

Template:

"Write a [genre] story about [topic/characters]."

Example:

Write a science fiction story about a robot discovering emotions for the first time.

7. Problem-Solving Prompt

Template:

"I am facing [problem]. Suggest [number] possible solutions."

Example:

I am facing procrastination in my studies. Suggest 5 possible solutions.

8. Teaching Mode Prompt

Template:

"Teach me [topic] as if you are my [teacher/professor]."

Example:

Teach me algebra as if you are my high school math teacher.

9. Question-Answer Prompt

Template:

"Answer this question in detail: [insert question]."

Example:

Answer this question in detail: Why do seasons change on Earth?

10. Checklist Prompt

Template:

"Create a checklist for [goal/task]."

Example:

Create a checklist for starting a YouTube channel.

11. Content Rewriting Prompt

Template:

"Rewrite this text to be more [style: formal / friendly / professional / creative]."

Example:

Rewrite this email to be more professional: 'Hey, I can't come to the meeting, sorry!'

12. Translation Prompt

Template:

"Translate this text from [language A] to [language B]."

Example:

Translate this sentence from English to French: 'How are you today?'

13. Analogy Prompt

Template:

"Explain [topic] using an analogy related to [field]."

Example:

Explain blockchain using an analogy related to a library.

14. Pros and Cons Prompt

Template:

"List the pros and cons of [decision/technology/idea]."

Example:

List the pros and cons of working remotely.

15. Framework-Based Prompt

Template:

"Explain [topic] using [framework/method]."

Example:

Explain marketing strategies using the 4Ps (Product, Price, Place, Promotion).

16. Persona Creation Prompt

Template:

"Create a persona for [target audience/customer]."

Example:

Create a persona for a 25-year-old software developer interested in AI tools.

17. Brainstorming Prompt

Template:

"Brainstorm [number] ideas for [topic]."

Example:

Brainstorm 10 creative startup ideas in the education technology space.

18. Code Writing Prompt

Template:

"Write a [language] script to [achieve goal]."

Example:

Write a Python script to generate Fibonacci numbers up to 100.

19. Debugging Prompt

Template:

"Here is my code: [paste code]. Identify errors and fix them."

Example:

Here is my Python code for sorting a list: [paste]. Identify errors and fix them.

20. Table Creation Prompt

Template:

"Create a table comparing [A, B, C] based on [criteria]."

Example:

Create a table comparing iPhone, Samsung, and OnePlus based on price, features, and battery life.

21. Step into Character Prompt

Template:

"Respond as if you are [fictional/real character]."

Example:

Respond as if you are Sherlock Holmes explaining how you solve mysteries.

22. Future Prediction Prompt

Template:

"Predict how [industry/technology/trend] will evolve in [number] years."

Example:

Predict how artificial intelligence will evolve in the next 10 years.

23. Exam/Test Question Prompt

Template:

"Create [number] exam questions on [topic] with answers."

Example:

Create 5 exam questions on World War II with answers.

24. Step-by-Step Guide Prompt

Template:

"Write a step-by-step guide on how to [task]."

Example:

Write a step-by-step guide on how to create a podcast.

25. Myth-Busting Prompt

Template:

"List common myths about [topic] and explain the truth."

Example:

List common myths about nutrition and explain the truth.

20. Top Prompt Engineering Tools & Platforms (2025)

1. PromptLayer

- **Overview**: A robust platform for managing, testing, and deploying prompts with features like versioning and advanced logging.
- **Ideal For**: Developers and teams seeking to track and optimize prompt performance.
- **Key Features**: Prompt versioning, API request tracking, replay dashboard for debugging.

2. LangChain

- **Overview**: A framework for building complex LLM applications, supporting prompt chaining, API integration, and memory management.
- **Ideal For**: Developers creating dynamic, production-ready AI workflows.
- **Key Features**: Multi-step prompt chains, vector database integration, logging and evaluation systems.

3. LangSmith

- **Overview**: A tool designed for logging and experimenting with prompts, offering features like chain tracing and evaluation tools.
- **Ideal For**: Developers using LangChain workflows who require detailed prompt analysis.
- **Key Features**: Chain tracing, evaluation tools, integration with LangChain.

4. PromptBase

- **Overview**: A marketplace for buying and selling high-quality AI prompts, catering to models like DALL-E and GPT-3.
- **Ideal For**: Users looking for pre-built prompts or wanting to monetize their own.

- **Key Features**: Prompt marketplace, monetization options, curated prompt library.

5. **Lilypad**

- **Overview**: A collaborative prompt engineering platform that supports tool-agnostic design and systematic prompt optimization.
- **Ideal For**: Teams and organizations aiming to streamline prompt development processes.
- **Key Features**: Collaborative design, tool-agnostic support, systematic optimization.

6. **Mirascope**

- **Overview**: A lightweight, user-friendly toolkit for software developers to optimize LLM workflows.
- **Ideal For**: Developers seeking a straightforward tool for prompt engineering.
- **Key Features**: User-friendly interface, lightweight design, LLM optimization.

7. **Haystack**

- **Overview**: An open-source framework for building search systems that can be integrated with LLMs for advanced querying.
- **Ideal For**: Developers building AI-powered search applications.
- **Key Features**: Search system framework, LLM integration, open-source.

8. **Guidance**

- **Overview**: A framework for building structured, reusable prompts with support for conditional logic and loops.
- **Ideal For**: Developers needing to create complex, structured prompts.
- **Key Features**: Structured prompts, conditional logic, loops.

9. **AIPRM**

- **Overview**: A browser extension that enhances ChatGPT with a curated list of prompt templates for various use cases.

- **Ideal For**: Users seeking to improve their ChatGPT interactions with ready-made prompts.
- **Key Features**: Prompt templates, browser extension, ChatGPT enhancement.

10. PromptHub

- **Overview**: A platform for discovering, sharing, and rating AI prompts, fostering a community-driven approach to prompt engineering.
- **Ideal For**: Users looking to explore and contribute to a community of prompts.
- **Key Features**: Prompt discovery, sharing, community ratings.

21. Top ChatGPT Models in 2025

1. ChatGPT-5 (OpenAI)

- **Overview**: The latest iteration from OpenAI, ChatGPT-5 offers enhanced conversational abilities, improved contextual understanding, and better handling of nuanced queries.
- **Use Cases**: Ideal for complex problem-solving, creative writing, and personalized assistance.
- **Notable Features:** Integrated into Microsoft 365 Copilot, providing seamless assistance across Word, Excel, and Outlook.
- **Pricing**:
  - ➢ **Free Tier**: Limited access with basic features.
  - ➢ **ChatGPT Plus**: $20/month.
  - ➢ **Pro**: $200/month.
  - ➢ **API:** $1.25 per 1M input tokens; $10 per 1M output tokens; $0.125 per 1M cached input tokens.

2. Claude (Anthropic)

- **Overview**: Claude is designed with a focus on safety and ethical considerations, making it suitable for sensitive topics and emotional support.
- **Use Cases**: Effective in providing empathetic responses, handling personal advice, and ensuring user safety.
- **Notable Features:** Recognized for its thoughtful and reflective tone, especially in emotionally complex scenarios.
- **Pricing**:
  - ➢ **Claude Opus 4.1:** $15 per million tokens (MTok) for input; $1.50 per MTok for output.

- **Claude Sonnet 4:** $3 per MTok for input; $0.30 per MTok for output.

3. Gemini (Google DeepMind)

- **Overview**: Gemini excels in delivering structured, analytical responses, leveraging Google's vast data resources.
- **Use Cases**: Best suited for research, data analysis, and tasks requiring high accuracy and detail.
- **Notable Features**: Demonstrates strength in rendering complex information with clarity and precision.
- **Pricing**:
  - **Free Tier**: Basic access with limited features.
  - **AI Pro**: $18.99/month.
  - **AI Ultra**: $119.99/month.

4. Perplexity AI

- **Overview**: Perplexity AI is known for its deep research capabilities, providing comprehensive and well-sourced information.
- **Use Cases:** Ideal for academic research, fact-checking, and in-depth analysis.
- **Notable Features:** Offers citations and references, enhancing the reliability of its responses.
- **Pricing:**
  - **Free**: Limited access with basic features.
  - **Pro**: $20/month or $200/year.
  - **Enterprise Pro**: $200/month or $2,000/year.

5. DeepSeek

- **Overview**: DeepSeek is an open-source AI chatbot that emphasizes transparency and customization.
- **Use Cases**: Suitable for developers and organizations seeking to build tailored AI solutions.
- **Notable Features**: Provides open-source access, allowing for greater flexibility and control.
- **Pricing**:
  - **Standard:** $0.27 per 1M input tokens (cache miss); $1.10 per 1M output tokens.
  - **Discounted (off-peak):** $0.07 per 1M input tokens (cache hit); $0.55 per 1M output tokens.

22. Top AI Image Generation Models in 2025

1. ChatGPT-4o (OpenAI)

- **Overview**: OpenAI's latest multimodal model, ChatGPT-4o, integrates advanced image generation capabilities, producing photorealistic and stylistically diverse images from text prompts.
- **Strengths**: Excels in creative and artistic image generation, offering impressive results in various styles.
- **Use Cases**: Ideal for users seeking high-quality images for storytelling, marketing, and design purposes.
- **Pricing:** Free tier available; subscription plans offer enhanced features.
- **Details**: While ChatGPT-4o is accessible for free, premium subscriptions provide additional benefits such as faster response times and priority access during high-traffic periods.

2. Gemini 2.5 Pro (Google DeepMind)

- **Overview**: Google's Gemini 2.5 Pro model is renowned for its precision and detailed execution in image generation, outperforming competitors in various benchmarks.
- **Strengths**: Superior in rendering complex lighting, motion blur, and achieving realistic compositions.
- **Use Cases**: Suitable for professionals requiring high-fidelity and technically accurate images.
- **Pricing**: Free tier available; premium plans start at $19.99/month.

- **Details**: Free users have limited access to Gemini 2.5 Pro, particularly for reasoning, math, and code tasks. Full access requires a paid subscription.

3. Recraft V3

- **Overview**: Recraft V3 is a generative AI model tailored for professional design workflows, emphasizing brand consistency, text fidelity, and layout control.
- **Strengths**: Offers high-resolution imagery and supports various styles, including photorealistic, illustrated, and vector formats.
- **Use Cases**: Ideal for designers and marketers needing consistent and customizable visuals.
- **Pricing**: Free tier with 50 credits daily; paid plans available.
- **Details**: Recraft offers a free tier that provides 50 credits daily for image generation. Paid subscriptions offer additional features and access to advanced models.

4. Flux.1 Kontext Pro (Black Forest Labs)

- **Overview**: Flux.1 Kontext Pro is a text-to-image model developed by Black Forest Labs, known for its high-resolution outputs and artistic rendering capabilities.
- **Strengths**: Generates images at up to 4 megapixels without affecting generation speed, suitable for detailed and candid photography styles.
- **Use Cases**: Perfect for artists and creators seeking high-quality, realistic images.
- **Pricing**: Free tier with limited credits; paid plans start at $9.99/month.

- **Details**: Flux.1 Kontext Pro offers a free tier with limited credits. Paid plans provide enhanced features, higher generation limits, and commercial rights.

5. Adobe Firefly

- **Overview**: Adobe Firefly is a generative AI model integrated into Adobe Creative Cloud, offering text-to-image and text-to-video capabilities.
- **Strengths**: Provides "commercially safe" outputs, making it suitable for professional use in marketing and branding.
- **Use Cases**: Ideal for businesses and professionals seeking legally safe and high-quality visuals.
- **Pricing**: Free tier available; paid plans start at $19.99/month.
- **Details**: Adobe Firefly offers a free tier with a set number of monthly generative AI creations. Paid plans provide unlimited access to advanced features and additional credits.

23. Top AI Video Generation Models in 2025

1. Google Veo 3

- **Overview**: Google's Gemini-powered Veo 3 offers cinematic-quality video generation with integrated voice acting, sound effects, and background music. It excels in creating realistic and detailed character models and scenes.
- **Strengths**: Supports seamless clip extensions and continuity, making it ideal for storytelling and cinematic projects.
- **Use Cases**: Perfect for creators seeking high-quality, immersive videos with dynamic audio.
- **Pricing**: Subscription-based, with additional AI credits required for extended usage.

2. Runway Gen-3 Alpha

- **Overview**: Runway's Gen-3 Alpha provides ultra-realistic video generation with precise key-framing and industry-level customization. It offers fine-grained temporal control and photorealistic human rendering.
- **Strengths**: Ideal for professional filmmakers and content creators requiring high fidelity and customization.
- **Use Cases**: Best suited for short films, advertisements, and high-quality video content.
- **Pricing**: Free trial available; custom pricing for enterprises.

3. Sora (OpenAI)

- **Overview**: OpenAI's Sora is a text-to-video model capable of generating detailed, dynamic, and emotionally expressive videos. It aims to assist filmmakers and creators with high-quality cinematic visuals.
- **Strengths**: Deep language understanding and multi-shot video capabilities.
- **Use Cases**: Suitable for creative professionals looking to generate complex video narratives.
- **Pricing**: Pricing details are not yet disclosed.

4. **Movie Gen (Meta)**

- **Overview**: Meta's Movie Gen supports video, image, and audio generation, creating immersive and personalized videos up to 16 seconds long. It also enables video editing based on text instructions.
- **Strengths**: Advanced storytelling capabilities with support for sound effects and music.
- **Use Cases**: Ideal for social media content creators and marketers seeking quick and engaging videos.
- **Pricing**: Pricing details are not specified.

5. Pika Labs

- **Overview**: Pika Labs offers dynamic video generation with camera and motion customization. It focuses on natural dynamic generation and is user-friendly.
- **Strengths**: Supports longer videos with frame continuation and is currently free during beta.

- **Use Cases**: Suitable for creators looking for flexibility and creativity in video generation.
- **Pricing**: Currently free during beta; pricing details for future plans are not specified.

24. Top AI Text-to-Speech Models in 2025

1. VibeVoice (Microsoft)

- **Overview**: VibeVoice is an open-source AI model developed by Microsoft that can transform plain text into high-quality, natural-sounding audio, including full 90-minute podcasts with up to four distinct AI-generated speakers.
- **Strengths**: Supports expressive voices, handles basic emotions, and allows for local deployment with models requiring between 7GB and 18GB of VRAM.
- **Use Cases**: Ideal for podcast production, accessibility applications, and AI assistants.
- **Pricing**: Free
- **Details**: VibeVoice is an open-source AI model developed by Microsoft that can transform plain text into high-quality, natural-sounding audio, including full 90-minute podcasts with up to four distinct AI-generated speakers. It addresses key challenges in TTS such as speaker consistency, natural conversational flow, and scalability. Currently, the model supports English and Mandarin, with plans for additional languages. There are two testable versions available: a 1.5 billion parameter model (64k context, 90 minutes) and a 7 billion parameter model (32k context, 45 minutes), with a lighter 0.5 billion parameter version in development for real-time use. Users can run the models locally, requiring between 7GB and 18GB of VRAM, or try an online demo.

2. MAI-Voice-1 (Microsoft)

- **Overview**: MAI-Voice-1 is a high-performance speech model capable of generating a minute of audio in under a second using just one GPU. It is integrated into services like Copilot Daily, where it recites news headlines and creates podcast-style discussions.

- **Strengths**: Offers expressive, natural-sounding speech and is optimized for real-time applications.
- **Use Cases**: Suitable for voice assistants, news narration, and podcasting.
- **Pricing**: Free trial available
- **Details**: MAI-Voice-1 is a high-performance speech model capable of generating a minute of audio in under a second using just one GPU. It is integrated into services like Copilot Daily, where it recites news headlines and creates podcast-style discussions. Users can test MAI-Voice-1 on Copilot Labs by customizing its speech content, voice, and style.

3. ElevenLabs

- **Overview**: ElevenLabs provides realistic and expressive AI-generated voices, including JARVIS, classic male/female voices, and voices suitable for speeches or children's stories.
- **Strengths**: Offers a wide range of voices and supports various applications, from educational materials to entertainment.
- **Use Cases**: Ideal for content creators, educators, and individuals with visual impairments.
- **Pricing**: Free tier available; paid plans start at $22/month
- **Details**: ElevenLabs offers realistic and expressive AI-generated voices, including JARVIS, classic male/female voices, and voices suitable for speeches or children's stories. The free tier provides 10,000 credits per month, which is usable for either 10 minutes of high-quality Text to Speech or 15 minutes of Conversational AI. Paid plans offer additional features and higher usage limits.

4. **Genny by LOVO**

- **Overview**: Genny by LOVO is a text-to-speech platform designed to deliver high-quality, expressive voice output. It supports asynchronous processing, generating audio in the background.
- **Strengths**: Provides reliable and polished voice results, suitable for applications that don't require real-time playback.
- **Use Cases**: Best for e-learning, audiobooks, and other applications requiring high-quality voice synthesis.
- **Pricing**: Free trial available; paid plans start at $35/month
- **Details**: Genny by LOVO is a text-to-speech platform designed to deliver high-quality, expressive voice output. It supports asynchronous processing, generating audio in the background. Users can start with a free trial to experience the platform's capabilities

5. **Coqui TTS**

- **Overview**: Coqui TTS is an open-source, Python-based toolkit for advanced text-to-speech and voice cloning applications. It supports a wide range of models and offers multi-speaker and multilingual support.
- **Strengths**: Highly customizable and suitable for both research and production environments.
- **Use Cases**: Ideal for developers and researchers looking to integrate TTS capabilities into their applications.
- **Pricing**: Free for non-commercial use; commercial use may require a license
- **Details**: Coqui TTS is an open-source, Python-based toolkit for advanced text-to-speech and voice cloning applications. It supports a wide range of models and offers multi-speaker and multilingual support.

The toolkit is licensed under MPL 2.0, allowing commercial use, but licenses of pretrained models may be different and are listed separately.

25. Top AI Speech-to-Text Models in 2025

1. Deepgram Nova

- **Overview**: Deepgram Nova offers ultra-fast, GPU-optimized transcription with advanced features like speaker diarization and real-time analytics.
- **Pricing**:
  - **Pre-recorded**: $0.0043/min
  - **Streaming**: $0.0077/min
  - **Free Credits**: $200 in free credits for new users
- **Best For**: Developers and enterprises needing scalable, real-time transcription with advanced analytics.

2. Rev AI

- **Overview**: Rev AI provides high-accuracy transcription with support for multiple languages and speaker identification.
- **Pricing**:
  - **Standard Transcription**: $0.005/min
  - **Human Transcription**: $1.99/min
  - **Free Trial**: 5 hours of free transcription
- **Best For**: Users requiring high-accuracy transcription with support for multiple languages and speaker identification.

3. Google Cloud Speech-to-Text

- **Overview**: Google's STT API offers robust transcription capabilities with support for various languages and audio formats.
- **Pricing**:
  - **Standard Model**: $0.006/min
  - **Enhanced Model**: $0.009/min
  - **Free Tier**: 60 minutes per month

- **Best For**: Developers and enterprises seeking reliable transcription with integration into Google's cloud ecosystem.

4. Microsoft Azure Speech-to-Text

- **Overview**: Azure's STT service provides real-time transcription with support for custom models and speaker identification.

- **Pricing**:
  - **Standard Model: $0.75/hour**
  - **Custom Model**: $1.50/hour
  - **Free Tier**: 5 audio hours per month

- **Best For**: Enterprises needing customizable transcription solutions with integration into Microsoft's cloud services.

5. AssemblyAI

- **Overview**: AssemblyAI offers a user-friendly API with features like summarization, sentiment analysis, and keyword extraction.

- **Pricing**:
  - **Speech-to-Text**: $0.37/hour
  - **Streaming**: $0.47/hour
  - **Free Tier**: Up to 416 free hours with API sign-up

- **Best For**: Developers and businesses looking for an easy-to-integrate transcription API with additional NLP features.

26. Answers to End of Chapter Exercises

1. AI: Your Friendly Neighbourhood Thinking Machine

1. **B) Talos, the bronze man**

   The text specifically names Talos, the giant bronze man, as an early mythological robot-like figure.

2. **C) Dartmouth College summer conference**

   This conference officially coined the term "artificial intelligence" with John McCarthy and others.

3. **C) It could learn and improve beyond its programmer's skill.**

   The text highlights that it eventually beat its own creator by learning from experience.

4. **B) It pretended to be a therapist through text conversation.**

   ELIZA gave early proof that computers could mimic human-like dialogue, even without true understanding.

5. **B) A network of "digital brain cells" that pass signals and adjust weights**

   The text explains it as computer neurons that turn on/off and adjust "weights" to learn patterns.

6. **C) Data**

   The analogy states: data are the ingredients, and the recipe is the algorithm.

7. **B) Deep learning**

The text names deep learning as the key to making neural networks far more powerful.

8. **A genius parrot**

   It stresses that GPT mimics language patterns like a parrot without true understanding.

9. **C) Predicting weather patterns centuries ahead**

   The text mentions spam filters, maps, and filters, but not futuristic long-term weather predictions.

10. **B) AGI (Artificial General Intelligence)**

    The text explicitly defines AGI as a machine that could learn and reason like humans.

2. What Is an AI Prompt?

1. **C) The input submitted to a large language model, such as a question or command**

   TechTarget defines a prompt as "the input submitted to a large language model."

2. **B) Student asking a question, teacher responding**

   The text says: "A prompt is what you say to the computer...just like you ask your teacher a question, you ask the computer something, and it gives you an answer."

3. **B) Predicting the next word based on patterns from training data**

   The text clearly explains that AI generates output "word by word" by predicting what comes next.

4. **B) A literal-minded but capable assistant who needs very clear instructions**

   The passage emphasizes that AI is "incredibly capable, but very literal-minded."

5. **C) Recipes illustrate the importance of precise ingredients and steps for accurate results**

   The analogy demonstrates that detailed prompts guide AI just as clear recipes guide chefs.

6. **D) Medical diagnosis**

   The examples were essays, travel, and cooking – medical diagnosis was not included.

7. **B) Because vague prompts make AI retrieve irrelevant or generic answers**

   The Flint guide is cited: vague prompts lead to generic or unfocused results.

8. **C) "Acting as a travel planner, plan a 3-day family trip to Paris."**

   This prompt includes a role ("travel planner") to guide AI's response clearly.

9. **B) Identical prompts lead to consistent style and subject in results**

   The demo showed that identical text prompts guided AI image generation toward similar results.

10. **C) Clear, specific prompts guide AI toward accurate and useful responses**

    The text emphasizes repeatedly that better prompts yield better AI answers.

3. What is Prompt Engineering?

Exercise – 1

1. **B) Because prompts, like code, are precise instructions that shape the machine's output**
   The text emphasizes that prompts "guide" the AI just as code does with machines.

2. **B) Saying "Explain this like a teacher" to influence style and tone**
   The text mentions role-based prompts such as "Explain this like a teacher" as examples of user control.

3. **C) Detailed instructions lead to results closer to the user's intent**
   The "ketchup sandwich vs. turkey sandwich with sides" story demonstrates this.

4. **B) They enabled models to process entire passages simultaneously for context**
   The passage notes Transformers allowed reading whole paragraphs at once.

5. **B) It demonstrates that broad instructions leave too many possible interpretations**
   The chef analogy shows vague prompts create ambiguity in results.

6. **D) Advances in symbolic AI rule-based systems**
   The text mentions data, computing, and algorithms — not symbolic rule-based AI.

7. **B) Programming tells the machine HOW to do something, prompting tells WHAT is wanted**

   This distinction is explicitly made in the text's comparison chart.

8. **C) Because knowing how to ask AI effectively is becoming as essential as reading and writing**

   The text directly frames prompting as a new literacy skill alongside reading and writing.

9. **B) The genie will misinterpret and provide unexpected or odd results**

   The analogy notes vague instructions to the genie lead to "crazy results."

10. **B) Programming builds the foundation, prompting decorates and directs usage**

    The text uses the house analogy: programming = foundation, prompting = decoration.

Exercise - 2

1. **a)**	6. **a)**
2. **b)**	7. **b)**
3. **a)**	8. **b)**
4. **b)**	9. **a)**
5. **a)**	10. **b)**

4. How Generative AI Understands Prompts

1. **b**

   Explanation: A language model doesn't "understand" in the human sense; it predicts the most likely next token given context.

2. **d**

   Explanation: Tokenization breaks words into smaller units (sometimes partial words), allowing the model to process language flexibly.

3. **a**

   Explanation: The AI "sees" only the tokens inside the context window; earlier tokens slide out of view if the sequence is too long.

4. **c**

   Explanation: A temperature of 0 minimizes randomness, making responses stable, factual, and repetitive if re-run.

5. **a**

   Explanation: A lower top-p shrinks the pool of candidate tokens, restricting diversity but increasing predictability.

6. **b**

   Explanation: Temperature = randomness dial; Top-p = how wide the probability pool is considered.

7. **d**

   Explanation: AI doesn't have real-world understanding — it predicts tokens statistically rather than truly "knowing."

8. **b**

   Explanation: Once the context window is full, older tokens slide out of view and are no longer available for prediction.

9. **a**

   Explanation: Even with a wide candidate pool (top-p = 1.0), low temperature forces the model toward the most likely choice repeatedly.

10. **c**

    Explanation: Frequency and presence penalties control how often the model repeats the same words or ideas, reducing redundancy.

5. Types of Prompts and Their Purpose

1. ***a***

   Explanation: Instructional prompts use imperative language to request a specific, well-bounded task.

2. **d**

   Explanation: The casual tone and back-and-forth expectation indicate a conversational prompt.

3. **b**

   Explanation: "List three benefits..." is an instructional, factual request—not an imaginative/creative task.

4. ***a***

   Explanation: CoT directs the model to articulate intermediate steps, improving multi-step reasoning.

5. **c**

   Explanation: The goal is an interactive dialogue that adapts via follow-ups—hallmark of conversational prompts.

6. **d**

   Explanation: Creative = imaginative generation; Conversational = human-like exchange. Different purposes.

7. **b**

   Explanation: The "think step by step" cue explicitly requests reasoning before the answer.

8. **c**

   Explanation: It's a clear, goal-oriented task ("Write an email..."), which fits instructional prompting.

9. **a**

   Explanation: Character/world creation is an imaginative generation task—squarely creative.

10. **b**

    Explanation: This statement correctly maps each prompt type to its core purpose.

6. Crafting Text Prompts for ChatGPT & Claude

1. **c**

   Explanation: Role prompting sets the "character" of the AI so it can respond appropriately to your context and audience. It's like asking an actor to play a role.

2. **a**

   Explanation: Assigning a persona ("cheerful travel guide") helps the AI maintain tone and style throughout the response.

3. **c**

   Explanation: System messages establish rules and boundaries for the AI, guiding its overall behavior across the session.

4. **c**

   Explanation: User messages are the real-time instructions or questions you give to the AI. They represent your requests.

5. **b**

   Explanation: Lower temperature settings reduce randomness and favor predictable, factual outputs.

6. **b**

   Explanation: Structured prompts help the AI produce organized, logical, and stepwise answers.

7. **d**

Explanation: The prompt defines both the role ("history teacher") and the instructional task, guiding tone, style, and audience.

8. **b**

Explanation: Top-p controls which words the AI considers, balancing creativity with predictability.

9. **c**

Explanation: Step-by-step reasoning improves clarity and coherence, but does not inherently ensure factual accuracy.

10. ***a***

Explanation: Combining role prompts, system messages, and appropriate temperature gives the AI direction, style, and factual reliability.

7. Prompt Recipes: Solving Real Problems

1. **c**

Explanation: Specifying both the **length and focus** guides the AI to deliver structured, actionable content rather than vague or overly general summaries.

2. **d**

Explanation: Role and tone (e.g., "friendly project manager") instruct the AI on **style, audience, and level of formality**, improving the relevance and professionalism of the output.

3. **c**

Explanation: Providing **context, the error, and the intended goal** gives the AI enough information to suggest precise fixes rather than generic advice.

4. **a**

   Explanation: Including irrelevant details confuses the AI. Clear criteria and structured instructions lead to **logical, organized pros and cons.**

5. **a**

   Explanation: Constraints on length and format ensure the output is **concise, focused, and easy to use**, particularly for summaries and structured reports.

6. **c**

   Explanation: Including **key content elements** ensures the AI writes a complete, informative email without missing important details.

7. **a**

   Explanation: Clear output requirements prevent ambiguity and let the AI **produce code that meets your functional expectations**.

8. **b**

   Explanation: Structured prompts with criteria and pros/cons allow the AI to reason logically and offer practical advice.

9. **b**

   Explanation: Iteration lets you tweak prompts for clarity, format, or focus, producing more precise and useful outputs.

10. **c**

    Explanation: Combining structure for coherence and role/open-ended cues for creativity balances accuracy with imaginative output.

8. Advanced Techniques

1. ***a***

Explanation: Few-shot provides mini-lessons with examples to teach the AI a pattern, unlike zero-shot.

2. **d**

Explanation: Showing examples helps the AI **understand format, tone, and structure** for tricky tasks.

3. ***a***

Explanation: Step-by-step instructions make the **AI's thought process transparent** and easier to verify.

4. **b**

Explanation: Asking the AI to **critique or audit its explanation** improves factuality and reliability.

5. **c**

Explanation: Iterative refinement **improves output quality** through repeated review and adjustments.

6. **d**

Explanation: Meta-prompts **turn the AI into a prompt coach**, guiding you to craft better instructions.

7. **c**

Explanation: Specifying the audience ensures the AI **tailors its response** to the appropriate knowledge level.

8. **b**

Explanation: Zero-shot is ideal for **simple or well-defined tasks**, where examples aren't necessary.

9. d

Explanation: Iterative refinement involves **incrementally improving prompts** based on prior AI outputs.

10. **b**

Explanation: Few-shot teaches the AI **pattern/format**, and step-by-step ensures **logical reasoning** is visible.

9. Prompting DALL·E and Image Generators

1. **d**

   Explanation: Being **specific with nouns, adjectives, and actions** helps the AI generate exactly what you imagine.

2. **c**

   Explanation: Adding **color, action, setting, and unique features** creates a richer, more accurate image prompt.

3. **b**

   Explanation: Think of it as **directing a photoshoot**; style, mood, and realism are like wardrobe, lighting, and pose.

4. **b**

   Explanation: Refining the prompt with explicit instructions and "no" statements prevents common AI errors.

5. **a**

   Explanation: Small prompt adjustments across versions help achieve the desired visual outcome.

6. **c**

   Explanation: Including verbs like "playing," "flying," or "leaning" tells the AI **what the subject is doing**, not just what it looks like.

7. **c**

   Explanation: Specifying **colors or tones** ensures the AI reflects the desired visual mood.

8. **b**

   Explanation: Concrete nouns, vivid adjectives, and clear actions help avoid vague or unintended results.

9. **b**

   Explanation: A **master prompt integrates all elements**—description, style, lighting, and placement—like a storyboard for a film scene.

10. **a**

    Explanation: Telling the AI **what NOT to include** helps eliminate common errors like unwanted objects or distortions.

10. Multimodal Prompting

1. **d**

   Explanation: Combining text, images, and audio gives **richer context and more nuanced AI responses**, improving performance on complex tasks.

2. **b**

   Explanation: The image **adds visual context** that complements the textual instructions, creating a layered understanding.

3. **b**

    Explanation: Audio input **provides emotional cues and speech patterns**, helping the AI produce nuanced responses.

4. **c**

    Explanation: Full multimodal prompts **combine all input types** for richer, multi-angle analysis.

5. **d**

    Explanation: Using images, audio, and text helps the AI produce **cohesive, visually aligned, and persuasive presentations**.

6. **b**

    Explanation: Multimodal inputs provide **visual, verbal, and emotional context** for more effective marketing content.

7. **a**

    Explanation: Combining **visual aids, audio narration, and text instructions** lets the AI co-create educational content aligned with the lesson.

8. **c**

    Explanation: Audio captures **human-like vocal nuances and emotional cues**, enhancing the AI's understanding of context.

9. **b**

    Explanation: Starting simple with a single mode, like **text + image**, helps users gradually learn multimodal prompting.

10. **c**

Explanation: Multimodal inputs simulate **human sensory input**, enabling deeper comprehension and more expressive outputs.

11. Prompting Other Tools: Midjourney, Stable Diffusion, Runway

1. **b**

Explanation: Style-based prompting requires **clear subject, style, mood, and environment details** to guide the AI accurately.

2. **b**

Explanation: Midjourney **picks up on expressive and mood-driven cues**, whereas Stable Diffusion is more literal and benefits from technical descriptors.

3. **d**

Explanation: This format **combines all essential elements** to get the AI to generate visually rich results.

4. **c**

Explanation: Fine-tuning **teaches the model your specific style**, allowing consistent outputs, unlike natural prompting.

5. **c**

Explanation: Midjourney **does not allow custom model training**, but you can build consistent styles using prompt tricks.

6. **a**

Explanation: Prompt libraries provide **tested templates and inspiration** that can be adapted for new creations.

7. **c**

   Explanation: Runway Gen-2 offers **prompt presets for video**, helping with transitions, themes, and motion cues.

8. **c**

   Explanation: Prompt libraries **serve as templates**, which can be adapted to produce **unique variations**.

9. **b**

   Explanation: Stable Diffusion **benefits from clear technical specifications** along with style, mood, and environment for precise outputs.

10. **d**

    Explanation: Effective prompting **requires clarity, creativity, and purpose**, enabling AI to produce consistent, visually stunning results.

12. Prompting for Business

1. **c**

   Explanation: AI copywriting works best when prompts provide context about the target audience, such as demographics, values, or preferences. This allows the generated content to resonate specifically with that group, rather than being generic or overly brief.

2. **b**

   Explanation: Prompting helps craft brand voice guidelines, messaging, and value propositions consistently, which ensures the brand identity is recognizable and relatable across channels. Manufacturing, pricing, and sales tracking are operational, not directly influenced by prompts.

3. **a**

   Explanation: Using overly technical or patronizing language alienates the target audience. Prompts must ensure the tone is respectful, clear, and approachable, which builds trust and ensures comprehension.

4. **d**

   Explanation: Long-tail keywords focus on specific search queries, making it easier to rank for niche topics with less competition, improving relevance and visibility. They don't guarantee instant top rankings and aren't directly related to aesthetics.

5. **c**

   Explanation: Customer personas provide insight into the needs, behaviors, and pain points of the target audience, enabling AI-generated solutions, messaging, or product features to be relevant and actionable.

6. **b**

   Explanation: AI prompting can quickly generate structured comparisons, such as SWOT analyses, allowing businesses to identify opportunities and gaps efficiently, but it does not replace human strategic decision-making or guarantee revenue.

7. **b**

   Explanation: Automating repetitive tasks involves using AI prompts to produce structured outputs consistently, saving time on tasks like emails, reports, or social media content. Writing unique descriptions daily without automation is not "automating."

8. **a**

   Explanation: A balanced content calendar addresses different audience needs and content types, improving engagement, brand consistency, and audience satisfaction. Viral posts and speed are secondary, and human review is still recommended.

9. **b**

   Explanation: Providing rich, context-specific prompts ensures AI outputs are more relevant and actionable, but human oversight is still needed. Vague prompts may produce inconsistent results, and fine-tuning doesn't make AI infallible.

10. **a**

    Explanation: The text emphasizes the APTR mantra: "Ask, Prompt, Tweak, Repeat," highlighting iterative prompting to optimize results, ensure accuracy, and refine AI outputs for business tasks.

13. Prompting for Education

1. **c**

   Explanation: Personalized tutoring works best when prompts contextualize learning with age-appropriate metaphors (like pizza), which aligns with the learner's cognitive level.

2. **b**

   Explanation: The text highlights adapting prompts to match learning styles (visual, narrative, step-by-step). Asking for diagrams explicitly supports visual learners.

3. **a**

   Explanation: The curriculum example demonstrates structured, age-tailored content with sequenced activities and projects—showing how prompts can guide AI to act like a curriculum designer.

4. **d**

   Explanation: Prompts can be tailored to provide not only cognitive support (knowledge) but also emotional encouragement, boosting motivation and engagement.

5. **c**

   Explanation: Embedding quizzes into a narrative (treasure hunt) leverages gamification, making assessments engaging while still testing core concepts.

6. **d**

   Explanation: Roleplay prompts simulate real-life interaction and allow AI to correct mistakes in context, which is far more effective than rote memorization.

7. **a**

   Explanation: Asking learners to translate sentences actively applies grammatical rules, reinforcing learning through practice, not passive reading.

8. **c**

   Explanation: Language is inseparable from culture. Prompts that include traditions, contexts, and fun facts help learners understand authentic usage and cultural relevance.

9. **d**

   Explanation: Adding humour through prompts transforms memorization into an enjoyable experience, increasing engagement and retention.

10. **b**

    Explanation: The text emphasizes that AI becomes a "super-teacher" when prompted to adapt explanations, design structured learning, and create interactive/cultural engagement—not because it replaces human teachers.

14. Prompting for Creative Writing & Content

1. ***a***

   Explanation: Effective creative writing prompts must supply genre, tone, and perspective. The vague prompt produces generic content, while the detailed one directs creativity.

2. **b**

   Explanation: World-building prompts should specify time, political structure, environment, and cultural context. This guides AI to produce a layered, believable setting.

3. ***a***

   Explanation: Providing character roles, goals, and conflict produces dramatic, natural dialogue. Generic prompts lack the tension needed for engaging exchanges.

4. **d**

   Explanation: Poetry relies on form and imagery. Clear direction on structure (e.g., haiku, sonnet), theme, and mood ensures stylistic accuracy.

5. **c**

   Explanation: Outlining prompts guide AI to generate organized frameworks that writers can expand, rather than unstructured paragraphs.

6. **d**

   Explanation: YouTube prompts must specify role, mood, pacing, and CTA. Aligning structure with audience expectations makes the script engaging and platform-ready.

7. ***a***

   Explanation: Social media prompting requires tone, brevity, hashtags, and emotion. The vague prompt lacks platform alignment and audience focus.

8. **c**

   Explanation: POV fundamentally changes narration and immersion. Without POV, AI defaults to generic storytelling that may not fit the author's intent.

9. **d**

   Explanation: Anthropomorphism (objects with human voices) plus tone/mood cues create rich, playful storytelling with clear creative direction.

10. **c**

    Explanation: The text emphasizes that effective creative prompts give AI clear roles, stylistic direction, mood, and platform relevance—unlocking creativity through structure.

15. Prompting for Software Development

1. **b)**
2. **a)**
3. **d)**
4. **b)**
5. **d)**
6. **a)**
7. **b)**
8. **d)**
9. **c)**
10. **a)**

16. Common Mistakes and How to Fix Them

1. **d) Hallucination**

   Explanation: The AI invented details about a non-existent book, which is the textbook case of hallucination.

2. **b) Verbosity/Redundancy**

   Explanation: Repeating "detailed" pushes the model to over-elaborate with circular phrasing and unnecessary fluff.

3. **a) Ambiguity**

   Explanation: The prompt lacks context, so the AI is forced to "guess," leading to multiple unrelated interpretations.

4. **b) Verbosity**

   Explanation: The response repeats the phrase "climate change is important" without adding fresh meaning.

5. **b) Demand the AI cite reliable sources.**

   Explanation: Asking for references or cross-verification reduces hallucinations by forcing fact-grounding.

6. **c) Hallucination due to false historical assumption**
   Explanation: There was no Indian Prime Minister in 1945, but the AI fabricated one because of misleading prompt context.

7. **c) "Give me an overview of the Java programming language, assuming I already know Python."**
   Explanation: Adding role, scope, and context resolves ambiguity by narrowing meaning.

8. **d) "Can you simplify this answer without losing meaning?"**
   Explanation: This trims verbosity while keeping substance intact.

9. **c) Because they fabricate false facts with high confidence.**
   Explanation: A wrong but confident-sounding answer can mislead decision-making critically.

10. **c) Structure prompts with clarity, context, and constraints.**
    Explanation: The root cure for all errors is precise, well-scoped prompting that sets expectations.

17. Tools to Supercharge Your Prompting

1. **d) Experimenting with versions**
   Explanation: Prompt libraries save time, but adaptation to new contexts (like language or audience) is essential.

2. **a) Review and combine AI outputs with domain knowledge**
   Explanation: IDE integrations act as assistants, not authorities; human judgment is key.

3. **b) PromptHero**
   Explanation: PromptHero organizes prompts into categories like writing, coding, and art, similar to Pinterest boards.

4. **b) Guardrails such as "stop if no relevant information is found"**
   Explanation: AI agents need clear stopping rules to prevent runaway processes.

5. **d) LangChain chains prompts, while AutoGPT plans and executes multi-step goals autonomously.**
   Explanation: LangChain structures workflows; AutoGPT acts like a self-directed agent.

6. **a) Learn the "why" behind prompt structures**
   Explanation: Blind copying skips the critical step of understanding how and why prompts work.

7. **c) IDE integration**
   Explanation: Real-time code completions in the IDE come from integrations like GitHub Copilot.

8. **c) It reduces context-switching by embedding AI into workflow**
   Explanation: Browser plugins integrate AI into the search process, saving time.

9. **d) Because agents may loop or pull irrelevant data if unchecked**
   Explanation: Complex agents need monitoring; small-scale testing prevents runaway failures.

10. **c) Prompt libraries → recipe books; Integrations → teaching assistants; Agents → project managers**

    Explanation: This matches the teacher analogies in the text precisely.

18. Ethics, Bias, and Safety in Prompting

1. **c) Red – harmful misuse**

   Explanation: Prompts encouraging hate or discrimination cross into *red-light* territory: stop immediately.

2. **b) Summarize a politician's speech neutrally for high school students.**

   Explanation: Responsible prompts focus on fairness, respect, and constructive goals.

3. **a) It avoids narrow stereotypes**

   Explanation: Broad, neutral framing encourages inclusivity and avoids bias toward a single model.

4. **d) Accepting the first output as the most accurate**

   Explanation: Bias detection requires scrutiny; blindly accepting the first answer prevents catching unfair tilts.

5. **c) Suggest careers for students based on interests, not gender.**

   Explanation: Neutral, inclusive framing avoids gender stereotypes and ensures fairness.

6. **b) Summarizing a confidential client contract in ChatGPT.**

   Explanation: Feeding sensitive business data into AI without security guarantees risks data leakage.

7. **d) Privacy protection**

   Explanation: Sharing personal health data without consent violates privacy and possibly legal rules (e.g., HIPAA).

8. **a) Asking AI to describe "a good leader" and it only lists men.**

   Explanation: This is bias-related, not malicious misuse; it requires caution (yellow light).

9. **d) Both shape perception unfairly by leaving out perspectives.**

   Explanation: Biased data gives an incomplete or skewed view, just like selective history teaching.

10. **c) Responsible prompts, bias awareness, and privacy safeguards = safer AI use.**

    Explanation: These three together form the wrap-up: responsible prompting, bias detection, and privacy protection.

19. The Future of Prompt Engineering

1. **b)**

   Explanation: Promptless AI means prompts fade into the background, as AI learns and anticipates needs from context and behavior — though corrections may still be needed.

2. **a)**

   Explanation: Just like browsers infer "http://" without asking, promptless AI makes prompting automatic and less conscious.

3. **d)**

   Explanation: The text warns that assuming preferences from yesterday (e.g., jazz music) may lead to incorrect actions today.

4. **c)**

   Explanation: Agents can chain multiple steps (e.g., research → analysis → presentation) and complete entire workflows.

5. **b)**

   Explanation: This goes beyond direct instructions, showing initiative by combining context (weather) with user needs.

6. **c)**

   Explanation: The Alaska vs. Spain example shows why oversight, trust, and transparency are critical.

7. **c)**

   Explanation: Orchestration involves designing flows between many AIs (vision, language, planning, decision-making) instead of relying on one model.

8. **d)**

   Explanation: Cognitive Design = designing *how* different AI systems interact to achieve outcomes.

9. **b)**

   Explanation: The text uses this metaphor to show how humans evolve from following set prompts to designing new AI interactions.

10. **a)**

    Explanation: The future isn't about disappearance but evolution — from direct commands to collaboration and orchestration.

www.ingramcontent.com/pod-product-compliance
Ingram Content Group UK Ltd.
Pitfield, Milton Keynes, MK11 3LW, UK
UKHW021404190726
13845UKWH00028B/879